19.95

FULLER/DIL · HUMANS IN UNIVERSE

# BUCKMINSTER FULLER
## ANWAR DIL

# HUMANS IN UNIVERSE

MOUTON

New York

A portion of the authors' royalties is donated to the
United Nations International Children's Emergency Fund (UNICEF)

**Library of Congress Cataloging in Publication Data**

Fuller, R. Buckminster (Richard Buckminster),
    1895–1983
    Humans in universe.

    Includes index.
    1. Fuller, R. Buckminster (Richard Buckminster),
1895–1983.   2. Technology—Social aspects.   3. Civilization.   I. Dil, Anwar S.   II. Title.
TA140.F9A36   1983        620'.0'.0092'4 [B]83–17451

ISBN 0-89925-001-7

Typesetting: Arthur Collignon, Berlin. Cover Design: Lothar K. Hildebrand
Printed in the United States of America.

First American Edition

Dedication

*To the wives with whom God has blessed*
*and inspired us*
*Anne Hewlett Fuller*
*and Afia Khatun Dil*

*And to the children with whom God has again blessed*
*and inspired us*
*Allegra Fuller Snyder*
*and Kamran Anwar Dil*

# Contents

*Front Cover*
Buckminster Fuller's Expo '67 Dome, Montreal, and Anwar Dil's "Ali" Calligraph 145 © 1980.

Buckminster Fuller                    Anwar Dil

*Back Cover*
Portraits by Antony di Gesù © 1983

# Acknowledgements

Our grateful thanks to: Kamran Anwar Dil for transcribing the tapes of many-houred conversation that has regenerated into the book, *Humans in Universe;* Dale G. Hamreus, Priscilla Norton, and Ann Emmons Mintz for helpful comments on part of the manuscript; Stefan Grunwald, Antony di Gesu, Nasim Dil, J. G. Bell, M. G. Rajah, and M. H. Usman for help in the initial stages of the preparation of the book; Abdelmajid Azzedine and Richard Chabior for help in library research; Wilbur T. Blume and Kiyoshi Kuromiya for arranging the meetings of the authors in San Diego; Jaime Lawrence Snyder for the meetings in Pacific Palisades; Kim Patterson, Lancie Chan and Evelyn Cummings for typing and work-sessions hospitality; and, Sandy Barnes, Ertunga Gemuhluoglu for general assistance.

Albert Einstein's letter and quotations are reprinted with permission from the Friends of the Hebrew University, New York. Quotations from Ezra Pound, Ernest Hemingway, T. S. Eliot, Christopher Morley, J. Robert Oppenheimer, Banesh Hoffmann, Muhammad Iqbal, A. J. Arberry, Pierre Teilhard de Chardin, Martin Buber, S. Radhakrishnan and D. T. Suzuki are reprinted with grateful acknowledgement to respective copyright holders. All quotations and their publishers are duly identified and appropriate credit given in each case.

# Prologue

## by Anwar Dil

*In 1934, when I was a child of five growing up in a small Himalayan town at the gateway to the ancient seat of Indus Valley civilization, comprising present-day Pakistan, Buckminster Fuller was already a well-known American design scientist who had created quite a commotion with a number of his inventions. Mrs. Eleanor Roosevelt learned to drive Fuller's Dymaxion Car and wrote about the experience in a newspaper article. H. G. Wells during his visit to the United States of America took a well-publicized ride in the Fuller Car in New York City. He told the thirty-eight-year-old inventor that he was familiar with Fuller's Dymaxion House, and later used some of Fuller's concepts in his motion picture* The Shape of Things to Come.

*About the same time, Fuller had submitted the typescript of his first major publication,* Nine Chains to the Moon, *to a leading American publisher who, in turn, submitted it to Albert Einstein for the verification of Fuller's rather bold chapters in which he had explained how Einstein's thinking process had led to his discovery of relativity theories and $E = mc^2$ equation. Early in 1935, Fuller received an invitation to go and meet Einstein who told him, "I am notifying your publishers that I approve of your conception of my thinking process."*

*When the book was published in 1938, Frank Lloyd Wright, the great architect, reviewing the work in* The Saturday Review, *wrote: "Buckminster Fuller — you are the most sensible man in New York, truly sensitive. Nature gave you antennae, long-range finders you have learned to use. I find almost all your prognosticating nearly right — much of it dead right, and I love you for the way you prognosticate."*

*Today, fifty years later, Fuller has come a long way with his mind. He is known world-around as the designer of the geodesic dome. His two-volume book* Synergetics: Explorations in the Geometry of Thinking *(1975) and* Synergetics 2: Further Explorations in the Geometry of Thinking *(1979), has been hailed world-embracingly by discerning scientists and men of letters as an epoch-making work destined to become one of the great classics of science. U Thant, Secretary-General of the United Nations, on reading the work called Fuller "one of those rare thinkers who can analyze the trends of human history and who is preoccupied with fashioning the future."*

*Fuller's twenty-first book,* Critical Path, *published in 1981, inspired the reviewer in the* Guardian *to call the author "a man so original that he had to create his own form of new-speak to match the scale and daring of his imaginative perceptions." Cautioning those who might be reading the eighty-seven-year-young Fuller for the first time, the reviewer observed: "Maybe the written language of the old, wise man is difficult, almost alien in the sense that highly original music seems at first alien. But what he has to say is actually humble and very simple, even if it is girded about with geodesics and mathematics and visions of men actually talking to men about their real needs."*[1]

*The reviewer in the April 17, 1983 edition of the* Sunday Standard *of Glasgow in neighboring Scotland opened his essay with these words:*

*Once in every age nature seems to produce a human mind which is able to function in an additional dimension. The list would include Roger Bacon, Leonardo, Paracelsus, Boyle, Newton, Einstein, and perhaps Tesla.*

*All, in a real sense, were mutants able to leap from conditioning thinking to direct contact with an intuitional reality obscured from the rest of us. Such minds crack open the current confines of knowledge and the world is never the same again.*

*Future history (if we have to have any) will probably elect Buckminster Fuller to the Society of Giants. Here in the Giant mould is a mind which seems extra-dimensional alike in physics, politics, architecture, philosophy and mathematics: the genuine polymath.*[2]

*The reviewer called Fuller's book "a plan designed to bring world opinion and world government to the point of cooperating with nature 'to accomplish what nature is inexorably intent on doing.' Which is to convert all humanity into one harmonious world family, sustainingly, economically successful."*

*In the world today, torn by utterly unnecessary, wasteful and degrading economic, political, religious and other rifts, we have few people who have the ability and the courage to speak to all aboard spaceship Earth, to use Fuller's own term — and fewer still, who if they do speak at all are listened to with respect across the national and ideological boundaries. It is important, therefore, to realize the significance of the fact that Buckminster Fuller is perhaps the only living American thinker whose integrity as a citizen of the world is universally recognized indeed.*

*In 1959, the United States and the USSR had an important protocol exchange. The USSR put on a major exhibition of their technology in New York to acquaint the American people with their way of life and work. Reciprocally, the United States sent Fuller's geodesic dome to be erected in Sokolniki Park in Moscow to house the American exhibition. Fuller was appointed by the United States State Department to be the engineering representative of the United States at the exhibition. While the large aluminum geodesic dome was being erected, Premier Nikita Krushchev visited the site. Next day the* New York Times *front-paged a picture of Krushchev on a scaffolding of the dome and quoted him as saying: "Very interesting, very good and worth copying many times over in the Soviet Union."*[3] *The Soviet*

*leader during his forty-five-minute visit kept exclaiming
about the Fuller dome and at one point, according to an
observer on the occasion, said: "Some American inventions are good inventions. This geodesic dome is a good
invention. I would like* Buckmonster *Fuller to come to the
USSR to teach our engineers." Subsequently, the USSR
purchased the geodesic dome from the United States. It remains in Sokolniki Park in Moscow and the metropolitan
subways advertise the Fuller geodesic dome as a worth-vis-
iting exhibit.*

*In 1964, Buckminster Fuller was appointed, along with
other prominent Americans, to represent the United States
in a joint meeting with a group of equally prominent Soviet
leaders to discuss problems existing between the United
States and the USSR. The American team, chosen by Norman Cousins and Patrick Moynihan, included, among
others, David Rockefeller, Norton Simon and John Galbraith. The Soviet team was picked by the USSR Academy
of Sciences. The meeting, that came to be known as the
Dartmouth Conference, was held for one week each in the
United States and the USSR. At the conclusion of the ses-
sions in Moscow and Leningrad, it was agreed by all dele-
gates that rather than having a summary of the conference
proceedings, one member representing each country
should present a discourse in the form of comprehensive
prognostications regarding human affairs in the world.
The head of the USSR Metereological Sciences presented
the Soviet position and Fuller was chosen to speak for the
Americans. Fuller was enthusiastically received by both
teams. At the concluding dinner party, the President of the
USSR Academy of Sciences said that henceforth Buckminster Fuller would be ranked in the Soviet Union along
with Benjamin Franklin and Thomas Alva Edison.*

*Fuller was first invited by the People's Republic of China
in 1953 to advise them with the structural strategies for developing their aluminum resources, but at that time he*

*could not go there. In 1979, Fuller was invited by the Chinese Secretary of Communications for a three-week visit. On arrival in Peking, Fuller was asked by his host: "How long would it take to make a complete disclosure of your general philosophy of the grand strategy of problem solving?" Fuller replied: "Sixteen hours." The Secretary said: "All right, we will start on Monday." The audience at the five-day seminar consisted of the members of the Communications Secretariat and the Chinese Academy of Sciences. Fortunately for Fuller and his audience, his interpreter was a Chinese scientist who had been one of Fuller's students at the University of Minnesota. At the concluding dinner meeting the Secretary of Communications gave a memorably short speech. He said to Fuller: "You are China. Please return."* The South China Morning Post, *the widely-read Hong Kong newspaper, in its edition of May 30 highlighted the conclusion of Fuller's visit with a front-page article entitled "US inventor takes China by storm." The newspaper reported the phenomenal attention paid to Fuller in China and that the Chinese people were eager to implement his ideas.[4] It might be significant to note that, according to a recent report, Fuller's 1963 book* Operating Manual for Spaceship Earth *is number one on the list of the ten most widely-read American books in the People's Republic of China today.*

*In India, as in a number of other Third World countries, Fuller's ideas are catching on. In the Indian mind, he is associated both with Gandhi and Nehru— a synergetic unity of the two. Jawaharlal Nehru had great personal affection and regard for Fuller's scientific and technological approach to upgrade the quality of the human environment. In 1969 Fuller was invited to present the Third Jawaharlal Nehru Memorial Lecture in New Delhi. Prime Minister Indira Gandhi in her introduction and welcome speech said that while Buckminster Fuller is described as an architect because of his special concern with living space, he is really an explorer of the architecture of the universe. Acknowledging his contributions through the geodesic dome and the dymaxion map, Mrs. Gandhi said: "But what is far more important is that Mr. Fuller has shown how to get the maximum from the minimum material by making the most intelligent use of the resources available on earth."[5] Fuller's discourse on the occasion, entitled "The Leonardo Type," is a thought-provoking exposition of the course of human civilization and the role therein of the Leonardo-type individuals who, to quote Fuller's own words, "grow to maturity without losing the full inventory of their innate, intuitive, and spontaneously coordinate faculties and therewith inaugurate new eras of physical environmental transformation so important as in due course to affect the lives of all ensuing humanity."*

*Fuller has travelled around the world more than fifty times and has lectured in more than five hundred and fifty colleges and universities on all continents, sharing his vision of the essential functions of the humans in Universe. Former Congresswoman and U.S. Ambassador to Italy, Mrs. Claire Boothe Luce, once wrote:*

*He has spent his life in search of the truths that make men free, but he has spent himself unsparingly sharing them with others − especially with young people. A passionate lecturer, he has excited and challenged the minds of generations of students, not only in America, but around the world. He has taught them that all human progress is the result of trial and error, of learning how to correct our mistakes. He pin-points with extra-ordinary clarity the technological mistakes our generation is making in handling nature, applying science for the benefit of society, and in using our own minds to the fullest − or perhaps one should say to the Fuller capacity. Bucky tells them how man can go about becoming what he ought to be, how he can create the good society − the society in harmony with both technology and nature.[6]*

*Mrs. Luce said very rightly that it is possible that perhaps Fuller will be best remembered as one of America's most inspired and influential educators. However, in my estimation, the most comprehensive assessment of Fuller's life and work was offered by Archibald MacLeish, three-time Pulitzer Prize laureate poet, playwright and author of many important books. MacLeish was Librarian of the United States Library of Congress, held a chair in journalism at Harvard University, and had served as Assistant Secretary of State in the United States Government. In 1978, MacLeish urged the President of the United States that Buckminster Fuller be awarded the Medal of Freedom. On that occasion he wrote: "Some forty years ago, I published, in* Fortune Magazine, *some views about the pioneering work of Buckminster Fuller in architecture, engineering and industrial design, which suggested to me that he was one of the most remarkable Americans in the latter years of the Republic— one of the very few by whom the greatness of our society would be judged. I am now convinced that this judgment fell short of the truth. If any man's life has reconciled our early spiritual achievements with our later scientific triumphs, it is his. And if there is a living contemporary who truly knows what it is to be an American, Buckminster Fuller is that man."[7]*

*On December 3, 1982, Buckminster Fuller arrived in San Diego to give weekend lectures as part of the World Game sponsored by the United States International University where I teach. I asked him if he would mind answering some questions which I had prepared. He agreed. The following day at noon commenced what proved to be a many-houred session covering wide-ranging topics. The conversation has resulted in the present book,* Humans in Universe.

*United States International University*
*San Diego, California*
*June 13, 1983*

# Humans in Universe—
# A Conversation

DIL

I want to explore with you how Buckminster Fuller, at the age of eighty-seven, as we move toward the twenty-first century, looks at himself as one who has lived through this century, and how his mind perceives this world and the universe.

But let me clarify my purpose in this exploration. I am interested in understanding how you look at yourself as a thinking individual human in the universe. But this is just a beginning, lest it become only a study of your mind, one human's mind. I am very much interested in seeing

*The thinking process*

through your thinking process how people like Albert Einstein, Leonardo da Vinci, and Buckminster Fuller think. I consider Buckminster Fuller's mind to be in the class of these people and I am interested in extending my understanding of the thinking process of such humans in our universe.

The first question that comes to my mind in this context is: When you met Ezra Pound during the Spoleto Festival of Two Worlds in 1971, he wrote:

To Buckminster Fuller
friend of the universe
bringer of happiness.
liberator.

How did you feel when he gave it to you? You have used it as the preface to your book *Intuition*,[8] so obviously it has special meaning for you. Could you recall the occasion?

FULLER

I and my wife had been visiting with Ezra and Olga in their very tiny little house in Venice. This was the point when he was first speaking to others, after the terrible time that he had after World War II was over. He had been captured and treated publicly as humans had not been treated by other humans in our century. It was in Italy where they first captured him and put him in a cage in the public square, and everybody was looking at this man in a cage. It almost killed him. He then had his St. Elizabeth incarceration in America, and he was so hurt that he stopped speaking. He apparently spoke to Olga, who was his companion, but not to others. And he had made a trip to Spoleto, for the annual festival. He had been invited to Spoleto because at the time of the music festival they had other events such as bringing ballets from around the world, and the committee at Spoleto had invited all the poets whom they thought well of, who were still alive, to come to Spoleto, and he was amongst the poets invited. He came in silence with Olga. Everybody was astonished when at the poets' performance in the theater, Ezra appeared on the stage with the other poets. When his turn came, he stood and read poetry of his own aloud. He had broken his silence. His voice was beautiful. The poetry was magnificent. His performance really jumped out from all the other poets, though some of them were very well known and had good poetry. But his performance was just what the whole cosmic level is about.

Then he was silent again after coming off the stage. Isamu Noguchi, the sculptor, and myself had lunch with him and Olga. We attempted to get him to speak by just talking to him, and he decided to answer us. He said to me: "Every time humanity gives me a chance, I make such a mess of it." He was in terrible pain. I kept on talking with him because he had apparently decided to talk with me. We then went independently to Venice after the festival was over and I met with him again. Noguchi was there and we had a very beautiful time.

Pound attends Fuller lectures in Venice

I went to Venice because I was invited to speak there. I was asked to speak on the Isle of St. Giorgio, where there was an old cathedral and its chapels. St. Giorgio was also a small modern navy yard, not the famous old Venice navy yard, but a secondary navy yard. There was a great chapel, and they asked me to speak in the chapel. I spoke there daily for a whole week. I spoke under the auspices of a number of Italian art patrons. They developed a combined school wherein individuals such as myself and Noguchi lectured first for one week in Florence and then one week in Venice. So this was the Venice week.

I was absolutely astonished to see Ezra in the front row. With half-hour breaks every two hours, I spoke throughout the whole mornings and afternoons for a total of eight speaking hours per day for a full week. Ezra was always

*Isamu Noguchi, Ezra Pound, Olga Rudge, Buckminster Fuller in Venice 1971.*

there in the front row on my left. I realized then that he was intensely interested in my work.

*With Pound on San Giorgio*

One day we went to San Giorgio and worked on a moving picture of Ezra, Olga, Noguchi, Priscilla Morgan, my wife Anne, and myself. While we were on San Giorgio, I saw in the background behind us some very extraordinary pine cones. On these pine cones the little ears that shingled down had edges of gold. So Ezra, Noguchi, and I in a very playful way talked about extracting the gold from the pine cones. And this was the kind of beauty of gold that was most valuable in the universe.

*With Pound on Torrello*

On another day we went to the very small island of Torrello. Torrello is an island that Hemingway was very fond

To. Buckminster Fuller
friend of the universe
bringer of happiness.
liberator.

With affectionate admiration

Ezra Pound

Spoleto
June 29th 1971

of. It has on it a lovely little church and a wonderful restaurant. The little church itself had extraordinary mosaic
murals. They were the best murals I had ever seen of all
the different disciples of Christ. They told much more of
their story than I had ever experienced before. Noguchi,
as an artist, and Ezra and myself whatever we were, felt
ourselves to be in the presence of really great art — very
mystically-inspired art.

Then there was the island's one little restaurant. At the
end of our luncheon in its garden they served pomegran-
ates. The patterning of the pomegranate seeds resembled
the pine cones. We saw them as rubies for our golden
pine cones. Their flavor was phenomenal. Following the

*Pound inscribes*
*canto for Fuller*

23

Torrello visit, he gave Anne and myself another of his cantos in which he wrote the following inscription:

*To Anne and Buckminster Fuller*
*in memory of the garden of San Giorgio*
*and the church of Torrello.*
*The gold from the pine cones —*
*The pomegranate.*
    *affectionately, Ezra Pound*
*eleventh October 1970*

It is a lovely piece, because Ezra is letting us know that he was happy again, after all the pain he had been through. He was really enjoying our company. It was a moment of mutual joy. It was soon thereafter that he wrote the lovely piece about which you spoke:

*Pound calls Fuller "friend of the universe"*

To Buckminster Fuller
friend of the universe
bringer of happiness.
liberator.

Then came a final talk at his own house. My wife and I visited with him and looked over and read from many of his cantos. As we left the house and were standing by one of the canals, about to walk over the bridge to take a ferry away from there, Olga ran out with this poem to me. He wrote it on the front page of his *Last Cantos*. When I got back to America and was doing my book on intuition, I wrote to him and asked if he would be willing to have me use his statement in my book. He said he would be very pleased by this.

DIL                    You must have thought that his tribute was a very elevating summation of your life and work.

FULLER                 It was a very beautiful day. You asked me what I thought as I received it. I was standing out there by the canal and his little house, one of a number of houses there. It was a tiny little three-storied marble-walled house. It was a spiral stairways with three landings surrounding a thirty-feet-high, vertically-tiered bookcase. Ezra and Olga apparently dwelt upon the tiny landings.
When the poem was handed to me I felt the skies becoming incredibly blue. The beauty of Venice and of the canal I was standing by and the beauty of my wife shone out. I felt a sense of comprehensive living. It was one of those moments when you have no other awareness than that of beauty.

DIL                    Marvelous! You have described it so beautifully.
*Pound captures*       Would you like to speculate on how he was able to cap-
*essence of Fuller's*  ture the essence of your life as a person and as a thinker,
*life and work*        in three lines?

FULLER                 I would not be able to talk about that except to recall that he had apparently exposed himself comprehensively to my thinking for that whole week. And a person who did

25

as much thinking as he did would have to have a whole lot
of exposure before he would be able to assimilate you in
his vein of thinking which was very profound, extraordinary. Have you read any of his books?

DIL

Yes, I have. You mention his *Last Cantos,* published in
1968, where in Canto 116 he says:

*Pound's* Last
Cantos

I have brought the great ball of crystal;
    who can lift it?

*Canto 116*

Can you enter the great acorn of light?
    But the beauty is not the madness
Tho' my errors and wrecks lie about me.
And I am not a demigod,
I cannot make it cohere.
If love be not in the house there is nothing.[9]

And from the final page of his last Canto 117, the haunt-
ing interplay of dissolution and integration in Ezra's
mind:

*Canto 117*

M'amour, m'amour
    what do I love and
        where are you?
That I lost my center
    fighting the world.
The dreams clash
    and are shattered —
and that I tried to make a paradiso
               terrestre.[10]

*Pound's poetic
significance*

Unquestionably, Ezra Pound is one of the greatest poetic
minds of our time. He is known as one of the inventors of
the twentieth-century poetic tradition mainly through his
recognized influence on T. S. Eliot, e. e. cummings, and a
host of other modern poets.

T. S. Eliot on
Pound's influence

T. S. Eliot in several of his essays acknowledged his personal debt to Pound for publishing his early poems in *Poetry* and later arranging the publication of his first book of poems by the Egoist Press in 1917. In 1922, Pound edited the manuscript of *The Waste Land* to about half of its original length, in the form in which it finally appeared in print. In the larger context of Pound's influence, T. S. Eliot said on a number of occasions that Ezra Pound exercised a vital influence upon English and American poetry, especially on the younger generation of poets: "Pound did not create the poets: but he created a situation in which, for the first time, there was a "modern movement in poetry" in which English and American poets collaborated, knew each other's works, and influenced each other. Who, I wonder, in England (to say nothing of the rest of Europe) read any American poetry written between Whitman and Robert Frost? If it had not been for the work that Pound did in the years of which I have been talking, the isolation of American poetry, and the isolation of individual American poets, might have continued for a long time."[11]

It appears, however, that Ezra Pound is more well-known in the context of particular political and ideological controversies leading to his indictment for treason against his country that he maintained he loved dearly. But what is perhaps of lasting significance is the fact that during his six-month detention in the airstrip steel cage in the Detention Training Center at Pisa, which as you say nearly killed him, he could write his *Pisan Cantos*. When the work was published in 1948 it was awarded the First Bollingen Prize in Poetry. In Canto 76, Pound says:

Pound's Pisan
Cantos

>      nothing matters but the quality
> of the affection −
> in the end − that has carved the trace in the mind
> dove sta memoria[12]

27

and in Canto 81:

What thou lovest well remains,
        the rest is dross
What thou lov'st well shall not be reft from thee
What thou lov'st well is thy true heritage
Whose world, or mine or theirs
        or is it of none?[13]

*Pound's Cantos*

Dr. Fuller, you asked me if I had read any of his books. I would like to say that I am a totally apolitical person. So, leaving aside Pound's statements regarding particular ideological and ethnic groups, and focusing attention on what he would like us to see as his "true heritage" to the world, I regard Ezra Pound as one of the finest poetic minds of our time. His explorations in his *Cantos,* on which he began work in 1917 and continued until his death in 1972, cover about eight hundred pages. They represent an odyssey of a truly original twentieth-century mind exploring the universe through representative cultural episodes of historical evolution toward a world civilization. For fifty-five years he kept working on what he jokingly called his "rag-bag of notes." In 1932, Ernest Hemingway observed: "The best of Pound's writing — and it is in the Cantos — will last as long as there is any literature."[14] I believe that future generations will appreciate his best work far more than we do.

*Fuller as explorer of human mind*

It is for this reason that I am particularly interested in Ezra Pound's assessment of Buckminster Fuller as "friend of the universe." He was himself a friend of the universe and I wanted you to recollect your meeting with him because I think as an outstanding explorer of the human mind himself he could unterstand what you have been trying to do through your explorations.
What Ezra Pound said about you, "friend of the universe / bringer of happiness / liberator," I really feel that this is

one of the most fulsome descriptions that have been made of your life.

FULLER    Well, in the line, "bringer of happiness," he liberated all the sense of happiness that I have ever experienced.

DIL    If you were to look back at Buckminster Fuller in another century or two centuries, do you think that in a short poem similar to Ezra Pound's you might like to say something about yourself? It would be interesting to see how your own poet's mind at this moment, projecting into the future, would look at yourself. I am interested in seeing what kind of parallel poem would come to your mind because you have an extraordinary ability to look at yourself objectively.

FULLER    I think I would be part of a universal mind, under the circumstance you just gave me, a few centuries from now. None of us knows what happens when we die. But I would think we would be part of a comprehensive mind. So our comprehensive mind would look at a single individual.
I think the most important aspect of myself that I know of is knowing how little I know. I have written a poem called "How Little I Know,"[15] I don't know if you have read it?

*Fuller's* "How    I have learned
Little I Know"    That man knows little
And thinks he knows a lot.
. . .
I am the most unlearned man I know.
I don't know anyone
Who has learned
How little one knows
As have I.

But that does not belittle
The little I seem to know,
And I have confidence
In the importance of remembering
How little we know
And of the possible significance
Of the fact that we prosper,
And at some times even enjoy
Life in Universe
Despite the designed-in littleness
That we have to "get by with."
. . .

Before Heisenberg, T. S. Eliot said,
"Examination of history alters history"
And Ezra Pound,
And even earlier poets,
Reported their discoveries
That in one way or another
The act of thinking alters thought itself.

When we ask ourself
"What have we learned?"
We feel at first
That the answer is "nothing."

But as soon as we say so
We recall exceptions.
For instance we have learned
To test experimentally
The axioms given to us
As "educational" springboards, and
We have found
That most of the "springboards"
Do not spring
And some never existed.
. . .

When man lacks understanding
Of nature's laws
And a man-contrived structure
Buckles unexpectedly,
It does not fail.
It only demonstrates that man
Did not understand
Nature's laws and behaviors.
Nothing failed.
Man's knowledge or estimating
Was inadequate.
. . .

I have learned to undertake
Reform of the environment
And not to try to reform man.
*If we design the environment properly*
It will permit both child and adult to develop safely
And to behave logically.

You and I
Are essential functions
Of Universe
We are exquisite syntropy.

DIL

*Fuller's Intellectual Development Game in "How Little I Know"*

I remember the first time I read "How Little I Know" as it came out in the *Saturday Review* (November 1966). I was in Bloomington, Indiana studying for my Ph. D. degree. I was deeply touched by a number of your ideas. I hope you won't mind my taking a few minutes in recalling your Intellectual Development Game which you outlined at the beginning of the poem.

I recall that
Thirty-eight years ago
I invented a routine
Somewhat similar to

Muscle development
Accomplished through
A day-by-day lifting
Of progressively heavier weights.

But my new intellectual routine
Dealt with the weightless process
Of human thought development
Which subject is
Known to the scholars
As *epistemology*.
And I have learned
That such words as Epistemology
Stop most of humanity
From pursuing
Such considerations
As the development
Of the thought processes.

So my new discipline
Was invented for dealing
Even with the ephemeral
Which word means
*Conceptual but weightless* —
As is for instance
The *concept of circularity*.

My new strategy required
That on successive days
I ask myself
A progressively larger
And more inclusive question
Which must be answered
Only in the terms of
Experience.

Hearsaids, beliefs, axioms,
Superstitions, guesses, opinions,

Were and are
All excluded
As answer resources
For playing my particular
Intellectual development game.

*Fuller's concept of Universe in "How Little I Know"*

Dr. Fuller, your conception of Universe as presented in this poem deserves quoting here especially in the context of Ezra Pound's tribute to you as "friend of the universe." I find it very helpful in understanding the overall framework of your thinking process.

The 20th century physicists,
In defining physical Universe
As consisting only of energy,
Deliberately excluded metaphysical Universe —
Because the metaphysical
Consists only of imponderables,
Whereas the physical scientists
Deal only with ponderables —
Wherefore their physical Universe
Excluded for instance
All our thoughts —
Because thoughts are weightless —

But thoughts are experiences —
Wherefore I saw
That to be adequate
To the intuitively formulated
And experience-founded controls
Of my ever bigger
Question and answer routine,
My answering definition
Of UNIVERSE
Must be one which
*Embraced the combined*

*Metaphysical and physical*
*Components of UNIVERSE.*

Thus my self-formulating answer emerged,
And has persisted unshattered
By any subsequent challenges
From myself or others
As:
"By Universe I mean:
The aggregate of all humanity's
Consciously apprehended
And communicated
(To self or others)
*Experiences.*"

*Man's function*
*in the universe*

On the question of man's function in the universe and also to understand your own life and work, the following provides a valuable insight:

I think man is a very extra-ordinary
Part of the Universe
For he demonstrates unique capability
In the discovery and intellectual identification
Of the operative principles of Universe · · ·

DIL        At this point I am going to take the liberty of requesting you to write a poem to Buckminster Fuller at eighty-seven with a century or two centuries of hindsight.

FULLER     Under those circumstances I would not be writing. I think the word writing is a term covering unique experiences we are having on board planet Earth before we die. We would be communicating in other ways.

DIL        All right, let us assume then that you are still on this earth . . .

FULLER     I would not be inclined to write a poem about myself.

DIL        Whatever you say in such a context might be a poem.

FULLER     I have also said human beings do not have the prerogative to rate themselves as being a poet. The term artist or poet, to me, can only be given to individuals by others.

DIL        You do write poetry, and you are a poet.

FULLER     I don't know — I don't call it poetry. And if you say I am a poet, that's all right, but I can't say I am a poet. I am not inspired by "myself." I can't write a poem to myself. I don't talk to myself. I have thoughts, some of which seem worth communicating to others. In 1981, I wrote "Cosmic Plurality," with illustration. I gave it to my friend Indira Gandhi.

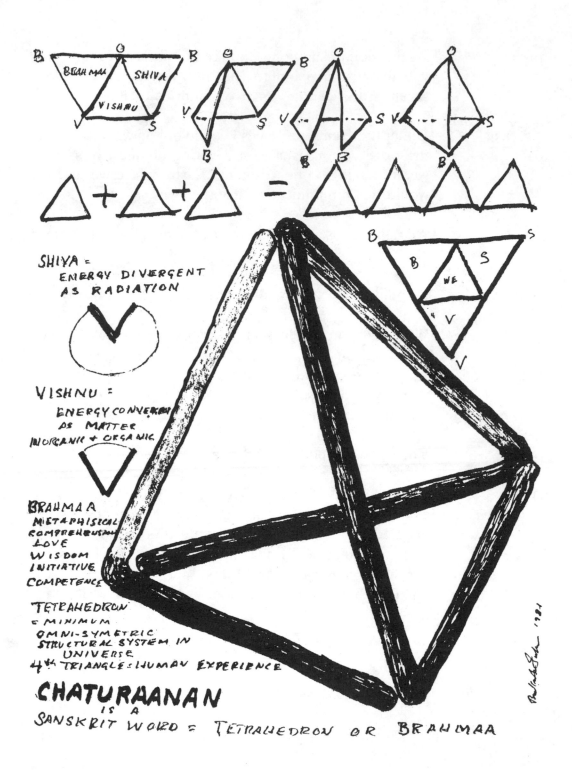

SHIVA =
ENERGY DIVERGENT
AS RADIATION

VISHNU =
ENERGY CONVERGENT
AS MATTER
INORGANIC + ORGANIC

BRAHMAA
METAPHISICAL
COMPREHENSION
LOVE
WISDOM
INITIATIVE
COMPETENCE

TETRAHEDRON
= MINIMUM
OMNI-SYMETRIC
STRUCTURAL SYSTEM IN
UNIVERSE
4th TRIANGLE = HUMAN EXPERIENCE

CHATURAANAN
IS A
SANSKRIT WORD = TETRAHEDRON OR BRAHMAA

*Indira Gandhi and Buckminster Fuller in New Delhi, October, 1981*

*Fuller's poem*  COSMIC PLURALITY

Presented to Indira Gandhi

Environment to each must be
All there is, that isn't me.
Universe in turn must be
All that isn't me AND ME.

Since I only see inside of me
What brain imagines outside me,
It seems to be you may be me.
If that is so, there's only we.

Me and we, too
Which love makes three,
Universe
Perme-embracing
It-Them-You-and-We.

New Delhi
October 8, 1981

37

There is something very special about you, Dr. Fuller, your ability to look into the working of the mind of a poet, an artist, a scientist, a thinker, an explorer. When you wrote your chapter on Einstein's 1930 essay on cosmic religious sense in your book *Nine Chains to the Moon*,[16] published in 1938, you were impressed by his nonanthropomorphic concept of God. You have called that essay the most important philosophic piece you had read until that time.

Einstein's thesis was that fear and longing are the motive forces of all human striving and productivity and thereby humans were brought to the cradle of religious thought and experience. You wrote in your book that Einstein had to reduce these two motivating forces to two words because he needed a polar terminology and that in your own interpretation these words were reducible to "Exclusion" (Einstein's "Fear") and "Inclusion" (Einstein's "Longing").

In course of time the religious sense developed into what Einstein called "the moral religion" because of the humans' need and longing for love and guidance. Both these forms of religion share the anthropomorphic concept of God. According to Einstein, only exceptionally gifted individuals in human history have risen above this level to display what he called "the cosmic religious sense" which gives those who experience it a marvelous sense of orderliness and oneness present in nature and the universe; and such people, among whom he mentioned Buddha, Democritus, Francis of Assisi and Spinoza, are inspired by a longing for "the totality of existence as a unity full of significance."

In Einstein's words: "No one who does not appreciate the terrific exertions, and, above all, the devotion without which pioneer creations in scientific thought cannot come into being, can judge the strength of the feeling out of which alone such work, turned away as it is from immediate practical life, can grow. What a deep faith in the rationality of the structure of the world and what a longing to understand even a small glimpse of the reason revealed in the world must have been in Kepler and Newton to enable them to unravel the mechanism of the heavens in long years of lonely work! . . . Only those who have dedicated their lives to similar ends can have a living conception of the inspiration which gave these men the power to remain loyal to their purpose in spite of countless failures. It is the cosmic religious sense which grants this power."[17]

*Fuller's 1934 commentary on Einstein's article* Your 1934 commentary on Einstein's concept of cosmic religious sense is insightful. In your view the condition of "Loneliness" that Einstein talked about was "L-One-liness" both at the macrocosmic and microcosmic levels of all scientist-artist-explorer experience, and that at both levels the scientist-artist is "a dynamically balanced, primarily longing-dominated being" and it is this cosmic religious or universe-embracing spiritual sense that underlies the cosmic ideas of a Kepler or a Newton.

Dr. Fuller, it seems that Einstein's thinking in this context has had a powerful impact on your own life and work, as you continue making references to him as a very special exemplar of creative ideas.

FULLER       I did not use the word "creative," though.

DIL          You did not. I know that you have a sensitivity to the term "creativity." You use it differently . . .

FULLER       I reserve the term *creativity* for the great intellectual integrity we call God. For humans I use the expression "conceptual realizations."

DIL          How would you say that Einstein's particular essay was so important in your life, or in your understanding the mind of Einstein?

Fuller's under-
standing of
Einstein's thinking
process

In your 1938 book *Nine Chains to the Moon,* you in fact proposed how Einstein had conceptualized time and relativity. It is an exciting story that created quite a stir during the thirties. You had written that working as a patent examiner in Switzerland, which led the world in the making of watches, clocks and other time-keeping devices, Einstein must have naturally thought a great deal about time. He must have been led to think that Newton had to be wrong in assuming a uniform and simultaneous time in the universe. Einstein's cosmic religious sense and his evaluation of time-keeping patents must have led his thinking to relativity and $E = mc^2$ equation. On your suggestion the publisher sent your manuscript to Einstein, who was so pleased with your understanding of his thinking process that he invited you to come and see him in New York. That means there is something very special going on in your own mind by way of your being able to understand how Einstein's mind functioned in terms of his "conceptual realization," to use your own term instead of "creativity."

FULLER

The word "pleased" I don't know about. What Einstein said was that he was advising my publishers that he approved of my method of ascertaining how he came to various formulations and he approved of my understanding of his methods of thinking. I think it was very extraordinary to have him say to me: "I am notifying your publishers that I approve of your conception of my thinking process." But he did not say it made him happy. He just said he approved of my capability to do so.

DIL

That is what I was pointing to: your capability to see how Einstein's mind worked on a particular conceptual formulation.

Would you say something more about your meeting with Einstein?

Well, that is the very essence of it right there.

A publisher had agreed to publish my book because a successful author, Christopher Morley, had recommended it. Six months later, I received a letter from the publisher's editor in Philadelphia, saying: "You have three chapters on Einstein, and we've looked up the list of all people that understand Einstein and you're not on it. In fact, we can't find you on any list. As a consequence, we think we must not publish your *Nine Chains to the Moon*. We want to avoid being a party to scientifically untenable speculation."

I was dismayed. Being also as yet young and a little bit "fresh" I wrote back to the publisher, "Dr. Einstein has just come from Europe to Princeton, New Jersey. Why don't you send my typescript to him and let him be the judge?" I had no hope that they would do such a thing, but nine months later my Woodmere, Long Island home telephone rang. The call was from a Dr. Fishbein who said, "I live at such-and-such an address on Riverside Drive in New York City. My friend Dr. Albert Einstein is coming in from Princeton this weekend to stay with me. He has the typescript of your book and would like to talk with you. Do you think you could come in?" Obviously, I accepted.

On Sunday evening I came to Dr. Fishbein's large Riverside Drive apartment. A number of Einstein's friends were already there. They were seated around the walls of an enormous drawing room. Einstein was seated at the far end of the room. As I was presented to him, I felt mysteriously moved. My reverence for him was such that I seemed to see a halo above his head. He immediately arose and excused himself and myself from his friends. He led me to Dr. Fishbein's study. On the desk of the study, under the lamp, I saw my typescript. We sat down on opposite sides of the desk. Einstein said he had read my typescript and found no fault. Better than that, he

41

said that he liked the way in which I explained how he happened to come to think as he did and how he had formulated that thinking into his relativity theories and equation. Then Einstein said, "I'm advising your publisher of my approval of your explanation of my formulatings."

*Fuller describes* Nine Chains to the Moon

I had three chapters opening my book. I am a comprehensivist and not a specialist. I am only natural like all human beings in that, and I did not get forced into being a specialist, thank goodness. I started my book working from the whole to the particular, with a tentative cosmic inventory in which I did inventory the limits of the macro-searching and micro-searching of scientists and the limits of technical realizations of those findings — to what height had man flown, and what did we know about galaxies. It was, incidentally, only five years before I was writing that Hubble had just discovered another galaxy. Up to that time we had known only of our own Milky Way. Hubble's 1928 discovery occurred just two years before Einstein wrote that cosmic religious sense article. It was a new idea that there were other galaxies, as noted in my 1933—35 Tentative Cosmic Inventory. Up to a week ago, i.e., January 1, 1983, the public knew of two billion more galaxies. Within this last week, you may recall seeing in the newspaper that with the new radio telescopes we have discovered two hundred billion more galaxies. So it is quite a difference between the tentative 1933 to 1935 and the 1983 inventory.

My 1935 Tentative Cosmic Inventory was so impressed with Einstein's 1930 piece on the cosmic religious sense that I wrote to the *New York Times* and to Einstein's publisher and received permission to use it to represent Einstein's philosophy. Then came my chapter of analysis of how he came to do his thinking. Then came a chapter in which I said that it is history that when a great scientist makes a breakthrough, the Academy of Science does not accept him right away. Einstein's theory determined how much energy there was in any given amount of matter. They never had a formula for that before. In 1933—35, Einstein's theory had not yet been accepted by the society of scientists. I said in my *Nine Chains to the Moon* piece that, personally, I was confident that in due course Einstein's equation would be proven to be correct; that after many years following the academics' acceptance, Einstein's theory and equation would finally get into the books in the universities and schools. When such new theories are proven and accepted, they provide a new kind of intellectual environment for the thinking of the children who are being educated.

I went on to explain in *Nine Chains to the Moon* that, within this new thinking, there comes invention of new technologies that take advantage of, for instance, electromagnetics, which would also take advantage of Einstein's theory that matter is energy. Then as the inventions are sold to various industries, industrial businesses begin to produce under the new technical knowledge. The inventions themselves alter the environment of society. Then, within that new environment, society behaves in certain new and unprecedented ways.

In view of this evolution, I wrote a chapter called "$E = mc^2$ = Mrs. Murphy's Horse Power." In this chapter I did my best to depict world behaviors predicated on my assumption that humanity would be behaving in accord with the philosophy of Einstein.

*Einstein's comment on practical application of his work* I will never forget the gentle way in which Einstein said to me: "This chapter about Mrs. Murphy. Young man, you amaze me. I cannot conceive of anything I have ever done having the slightest practical application. I have explored, hoping that what I find might be useful to astrophysicists, to cosmogonists, but practical applications are not anticipated."

*Albert Einstein and J. Robert Oppenheimer (Director of Manhattan Project)*

*"Late in his life, in connection with his despair over weapons and wars, Einstein said that if he had to live it over again he would be a plumber. This was a balance of seriousness and jest that no one should now attempt to disturb. Believe me, he had no idea of what it was to be a plumber, least of all in the United States, where we have a joke that the typical behaviour of this specialist is that he never brings his tools to the scene of the crisis. Einstein brought his tools to his crises: Einstein was a physicist, a natural philosopher, the greatest of our time. . . .*

44

*Einstein is often blamed or praised or credited with these miserable bombs. It is not in my opinion true. The special theory of relativity might not have been beautiful without Einstein; but it would have been a tool for physicists, and by 1932 the experimental evidence for the inter-convertibility of matter and energy which he had predicted was overwhelming. The feasibility of doing anything with this in such a massive way was not clear until seven years later, and then almost by accident. This was not what Einstein really was after. His part was that of creating an intellectual revolution, and discovering more than any scientist of our time how profound were the errors made by men before them.*"[18]

*— J. Robert Oppenheimer's "On Albert Einstein," in a commemoration of Einstein's 10th death anniversary in 1965.*

Manhattan
Project

It was two years after he said that to me that Hahn and Strassmann in Germany discovered theoretical fission — they were aided by Lisa Meitner. They communicated by secret messenger to their New York scientist colleagues, confiding that they had found theoretical fission. They were also confident that Hitler's scientists were seeking that atomic energy breakthrough. Hahn and Strassmann's German-Jewish scientist friends in America calculated their work and sure enough, they confirmed Hahn and Strassmann's discovery. Their New York scientist friends then said that nobody would believe their discovery in the political world. Franklin Roosevelt would not believe an unknown name to him, but he might accredit Einstein if Einstein notified him that theoretical fission had occurred. Einstein agreed to do it. President Roosevelt had been given an emergency fund by the New Deal congress. He had enormous funds not used. He took eighty billion dollars of it and applied it immediately to what eventually became known as the Manhattan Project. Out of all this came the physically successful Fermi

45

Albert Einstein
Old Grove Rd.
Nassau Point
Peconic, Long Island

August 2nd, 1939

F.D. Roosevelt,
President of the United States,
White House
Washington, D.C.


Sir:

Some recent work by E.Fermi and L. Szilard, which has been communicated to me in manuscript, leads me to expect that the element uranium may be turned into a new and important source of energy in the immediate future. Certain aspects of the situation which has arisen seem to call for watchfulness and, if necessary, quick action on the part of the Administration. I believe therefore that it is my duty to bring to your attention the following facts and recommendations:

In the course of the last four months it has been made probable - through the work of Joliot in France as well as Fermi and Szilard in America - that it may become possible to set up a nuclear chain reaction in a large mass of uranium, by which vast amounts of power and large quantities of new radium-like elements would be generated. Now it appears almost certain that this could be achieved in the immediate future.

This new phenomenon would also lead to the construction of bombs, and it is conceivable - though much less certain - that extremely powerful bombs of a new type may thus be constructed. A single bomb of this type, carried by boat and exploded in a port, might very well destroy the whole port together with some of the surrounding territory. However, such bombs might very well prove to be too heavy for transportation by air.

The United States has only very poor ores of uranium in moderate quantities. There is some good ore in Canada and the former Czechoslovakia, while the most important source of uranium is Belgian Congo.

In view of this situation you may think it desirable to have some permanent contact maintained between the Administration and the group of physicists  working on chain reactions in America. One possible way of achieving this might be for you to entrust with this task a person who has your confidence and who could perhaps serve in an inofficial capacity. His task might comprise the following:

a) to approach Government Departments, keep them informed of the further development, and put forward recommendations for Government action giving particular attention to the problem of securing a supply of uranium ore for the United States;

b) to speed up the experimental work,which is at present being carried on within the limits of the budgets of University laboratories, by providing funds, if such funds be required, through his contacts with private persons who are willing to make contributions for this cause, and perhaps also by obtaining the co-operation of industrial laboratories which have the necessary equipment.

I understand that Germany has actually stopped the sale of uranium from the Czechoslovakian mines which she has taken over. That she should have taken such early action might perhaps be understood on the ground that the son of the German Under-Secretary of State, von Weizsäcker, is attached to the Kaiser-Wilhelm-Institut in Berlin where some of the American work on uranium is now being repeated.

Yours very truly,

A. Einstein

(Albert Einstein)

pile which proved Einstein's equation to be correct. For the first time in history, the amount of energy in a given amount of matter was being accurately anticipated.

Einstein on atomic bomb

Having heard Einstein say to me that he had never expected any practical application of his work, I could correctly imagine Einstein's feelings in having his theories finding their first practical application on Hiroshima. I know the old man was really broken over this for the rest of his life. And, in fact, with it he discovered, and he let all his friends know that this experience quite clearly demonstrated, that scientists were caged birds with the system encouraging them to lay eggs; the disposition of the eggs became the exclusive prerogative of the powerful people. And the powerful people would take away those eggs and the scientific people would have nothing to do with what happened to them.

DIL
This gives us a sobering insight into what the role of the scientist, the thinker, the artist, is in our time.

Einstein as artist using the medium of science

Going back to our exploration of the way Einstein's mind worked, some people say that he was an artist who was using the medium of science to do his thinking . . .

FULLER
I didn't say that.

DIL
No, the physicist Banesh Hoffmann, who was Einstein's assistant in 1937, did. In his book *Albert Einstein, Creator and Rebel,* that won the 1973 Science Writing Award of the American Institute of Physics, Hoffmann noted: "He was at heart an artist, employing the medium of science."[19] You wouldn't say that, would you?

FULLER
I don't say that.

DIL
What would you say?

FULLER
I would say the word "scientist," the word "artist," the word "poet," are invented by humans.

DIL

In your essay "The Leonardo Type," which was your discourse as the Third Jawaharlal Nehru Memorial Lecturer in New Dehli, 1969, you wrote: "Ralph Waldo Emerson defined poetry as 'saying the most important things in the simplest way.' By that definition Einstein became and will probably remain history's greatest poet — for who could say so much so simply as did Einstein when he described physical Universe as $E = mc^2$?"[20]

Do you have any other recollections of Einstein?

FULLER

*Einstein visits
Fuller's geodesic
tensegrity project*

I often saw Einstein on the streets of Princeton in 1951 through 1954. I and other Princeton people respected him so much that none of us ever introduced or reintroduced ourselves to him in the street. I never stopped him and said, "I'm the man who said such-and-such to you in 1935." But I did have a fascinating indirect encounter in 1953.

In the 1950s Princeton's architectural department had an experimental station near the university stadium. In the years before World War I, the building had been used as the Princeton polo team's stables and dressing rooms. As an architectural student project conducted by me, we erected a fifty-foot-diameter model of my geodesic tensegrity sphere. It was made of ninety aluminum tubes and flexible, aircraft stainless steel cables. Einstein walked over to study it. I wasn't there at the time but was told by the architectural students and faculty who were there that he was extraordinarily moved by it.

I feel that a person like Einstein is tremendously sensitive in trying to understand: "What is Universe? What is going on in the universe? How come Universe? What am I to think and do about being included in the universe?" I am confident that such questions stirred Einstein's thoughts and motivated his work.

I am sure that is the reason Ezra Pound said "friend of the universe" about me.

49

Little children marvel at the universe. Those are the kinds of thoughts we have when we first recollect having thoughts. With the mysterious experience of being loved and looking around, we enter the era which we first remember. We remember just that we were fascinated with the universe. A child looks at the sky and understands it, looks at the trees, looks at the snow falling and sees that the snowflakes are all hexagonal, always cosmically-perfect patterns. These are the simple perfections of every child's experience. Every child is a poet. In 1922, Christopher Morley wrote a poem about this:

## To a Child

The greatest poem ever known,
Is one all poets have outgrown:
The poetry, innate, untold,
Of being only four years old.

Still young enough to be a part
Of Nature's great impulsive heart,
Born comrade of bird, beast and tree
And unselfconscious as the bee —

And yet with lovely reason skilled
Each day new paradise to build;
Elate explorer of each sense,
Without dismay, without pretense!

In your unstained transparent eyes
There is no conscience, no surprise:
Life's queer conundrums you accept,
Your strange divinity still kept.

Being, that now absorbs you, all
Harmonious, unit, integral,
Will shred into perplexing bits, —
Oh, contradictions of the wits!

And Life, that sets all things in rhyme,
May make you poet, too, in time —
But there were days, O tender elf,
When you were Poetry itself![21]

DIL

*Tagore's poem to a
child*

I am here reminded of a poem by the Nobel-Laureate Rabindranath Tagore. My wife, Afia, is from Dhaka, Bangladesh. I remember her reciting the original poem in Bengali to our son, Kamran, when he was a little boy, and to her daughters, Shaheen and Saeqa, who grew up as my own. We all used to have lots of fun together with Tagore's poem which I think is one of the loveliest poems to a child. In Afia's translation it reads like this:

## To a Child

The child calls his mother and asks:
"Where did I come from, Mother?
Where did you find me?"

The Mother smiles and cries,
    takes the child in her arms and says:
You were the desire in my heart!
You were in my childhood play of dolls.
Every morning as I prayed to Shiva
I shaped you and reshaped you
You were with my god on his throne,
And adoring him I adored you.

In my hope of all times and in all my love
In the heart of my mother and my grandmother
In this old house of ours,
    in the lap of our house-goddess
God knows how long you were in hiding.
When in my youth I had the awakening
You were the fragrance within me
You were there in my young body
With all your tender loveliness.

*Rabindranath Tagore*

You are the treasure of all gods,
    You are the perennial love of Eternal Time
You are as timeless as the morning light
From all the dreams of the world
    You came in a stream of joy
Bringing happiness in your mother's heart.

I look and keep on looking at you
    and do not understand the mystery that you are
You belong to the world
    How did you come to be mine?
How this little body of yours kissed mine
    and became the Mother's Child;
How did you appear in the world with beautiful smiles?
That is why I am sometimes so frightened
    I want to keep you in my heart —
I die crying when you are away —
I do not know with what net of love should I tie
    this treasure of the universe,
And keep it in my two weak arms!


Translated from the original
in Bengali by Afia Dil

FULLER

Alexandra, Anne's and my first child, born in 1918 just after World War I, caught the flu, infantile paralysis, spinal meningitis, and died of pneumonia on her fourth birthday. Our second daughter Allegra, born five years after Alexandra's death, was wonderfully healthy and happy. She named her daughter Alexandra after her sister. Alexandra, our grand-daughter, is a year and a half older than our grandson Jamie Lawrence Snyder. On his eleventh birthday I came into Jamie's room and saw on his desk a sheet of paper written by Alexandra. Tagore's lines:

You belong to the world
How did you come to be mine?

make me think of and wish to repeat Alexandra's poem to Jamie:

*Fuller with his grandchildren Jamie and Alexandra Snyder, 1959.*

So many love you,
As do I
Who do I thank
On this day of your birth?
That you were born
A part of me
That you were born
My brother.

*Earliest childhood memories of the universe*

So the word poetry does relate to that extraordinary moment of earlier experiences we try to remember, as we begin to emerge from our mothers' arms and being loved and being suckled. I cannot remember being suckled, maybe you can, I cannot — but I do remember so much of the smell of the air, the freshness of the gardens, the way

*Fuller and his daughter Allegra during the celebration of his 70th birthday in Greece, 1965.*

the tops of trees were moving around, how extraordinary it is, that blue sky, and as they say, snow coming, rain falling on the ground, and all those things. And I am sure all children feel all that. Then someone says: "Now, you have got to go to school, we have to teach you something,

*"The most poetical experiences of my life have been those moments of conceptual comprehension of a few of the extraordinary generalized principles and their complex interactions that are apparently employed in the governance of universal evolution."*
*— Fuller lecturing under the auspices of the United States International University, San Diego, December 3, 1982.*

pay attention." The system tells you to pay no further attention to your own original thinking about the interrelated significance of directly-experienced phenomena. I was told by my mother, who I was sure loved me, "Darling, never mind what you think — listen — we are trying to teach you." All the school teachers said the same thing to me. Knowing how dearly my mother loved me, I did my best not to listen to my own thoughts.
As I said, every child is a friend of the universe, and I, as an original friend of the universe having temporarily lost that friendship, have now pretty much recaptured it. I have done everything I could to unfetter myself from all

the social impositions. I apparently have purged myself pretty thoroughly of the erroneous thinking and value systems that society has put on its young about the explanations of life and the games the teachers play. I am pretty well free of those.

Last night you came to listen to me speaking before a university audience. I would not be dealing in tetrahedra and octahedra and icosahedra as the three basic structural systems of Universe if I had gone along with the schools' geometric teaching wherein everything goes back to squares and cubes.

DIL

*Einstein's view of the world*

It is interesting that when Einstein was asked to look back at his life, he wrote about the phenomenon you are talking about: "Out yonder there was this huge world, which exists independently of us human beings and which stands before us like a great, eternal riddle, at least partially accessible to our inspection and thinking. The contemplation of this world beckoned like a liberation, and I soon noticed that many a man whom I had learned to esteem and to admire had found inner freedom and security in devoted occupation with it. The mental grasp of this extra-personal world within the frame of the given possibilities swam as highest aim half consciously and half unconsciously before my mind's eye. Similarly motivated men of the present and of the past, as well as the insights which they had achieved, were the friends which could not be lost."[22]

In essence, this is the same idea you have developed in your writings, probably independently of Einstein. And this fact interests me greatly because we need such inspired humans, in growing numbers, to inhabit the future.

FULLER

I think Einstein was fortunate in that he probably never lost his childhood. I temporarily had mine taken away from me.

*Sketch of Einstein by Leonid Pasternak, the father of Boris Pasternak.
Courtesy of Lydia Slater-Pasternak.*

*"Music does not* influence *research work, but both are nourished by the same
source of longing, and they complement one another in the release they offer."*
— *Albert Einstein in a letter to a correspondent, October 23, 1928.*

*Quoted in* Albert Einstein: The Human Side; New Glimpses from his Archives, *Selected and edited by Helen Dukas and Banesh Hoffmann. Princeton, New Jersey: Princeton University Press, 1979, p. 78.*

| | |
|---|---|
| DIL | Very temporarily — for a very short time. |
| FULLER<br><br>*Fuller's childhood* | I know. And I had to unburden myself from that. I had a personality put upon me of how my school wanted me to be. And what my mother wanted me to be. She wanted me to be a success in the world of the business game. She was a darling and out of her love she did not want me to be hurt. She wanted me to be a success in it. But she became more and more fearful that I was going to be more and more in great trouble. She also said that she was afraid that I was going to go to the penitentiary. Because of my initiatives, the things I did got me into trouble with society. Robin Hood was my hero. Whenever I found individuals in trouble I felt completely free to operate transcendentally to man-made laws, so I did have to go through a great deal to throw off the superficial mantle that was on me. When not Robinhooding, I tried to behave in ways that were pleasing to my mother, which was playing a role which was not me at all. You understand me? |
| DIL | Yes I do, very much so — from my own experience. |
| FULLER | I don't think Einstein ever went through anything like that. |
| DIL | Maybe, perhaps not to that extent, but he did, of course. |
| FULLER<br>*All children born*<br>*as geniuses* | But my point is that whatever you speak about that people have or Einstein had or I have, I am saying every child is born with. |
| DIL | Oh, yes, I believe that. |
| FULLER | I have often written that children, all children, are born geniuses and get de-geniused very rapidly by the fear and love of their parents that they won't fit into the system, that the power system will hurt them. |

DIL

Still the question remains, even though every child is born with the capacity to be a genius and to function like one, how does the mind of people like Albert Einstein and Buckminster Fuller work? And that is one reason I was hoping that you would speak a little on how Einstein's mind worked by way of what precisely *thinking* is. What I am hoping to do by pursuing this question is to try to understand, through your interpretation of what Einstein said in his autobiographical notes, from which I have quoted earlier.

*Einstein's view of what precisely is thinking*

Einstein regarded this as a critical question in his reflections on life and observed: "What precisely, is 'thinking'? When, at the reception of sense-impressions, memory-pictures emerge, this is not yet 'thinking'. And when such pictures form series, each member of which calls forth another, this too is not yet 'thinking'. When, however, a certain picture turns up in many such series, then — precisely through such return — it becomes an ordering element for such series, in that it connects series which in themselves are unconnected. Such an element becomes an instrument, a concept. I think that the transition from free association or 'dreaming' to thinking is characterized by the more or less dominating role which the 'concept' plays in it. It is by no means necessary that a concept must be connected with a sensorily cognizable and reproducible sign (word); but when this is the case thinking becomes by means of that fact communicable."[23]

FULLER

*Brain and mind*

Last night I differentiated for you brain and mind. Brain, relating to the images that Einstein speaks about, the brain is dealing in images and experiences. I said mind and mind alone has the capability from time to time to discover relationships existing between the special case — brain conceptionings. Einstein says something in what you have just read to me, very close to something I have just said.

I say the following, too, sir. All the time we are having experiences, and they may be while just drinking our tea, or whatever it is, we do not think anything about that — we drink tea many times. But there comes a moment when I am experiencing something — which it seems to me I have experienced before, that is all you can say. Then comes another experience when this seems to be the experience that I said a while back that I thought I had experienced before — this is the third case. And if I am thinking, I ask myself, "How long ago was that last time?" I could not go back to the first "I think of" experiences, because I did not know at that time that what I was experiencing had any significance whatsoever. I can go back to the third time of experiencing something when I said, "I think what I am now experiencing I have experienced before; and that was just three months ago."

If there is some periodic significance in what I am thinking about what I am feeling, then there is some significant factor in my thinking that I have had this experience before, which is repeating itself embodied in some other experience; then three months from today I will be liable to have the same kind of experience and thought. Three months from today when it happens, I say, "I have really discovered something. What is it?" then I begin to think. It takes literally four experiences for mind to discover that there is an interrelationship significance going on here that was not to be evidenced in one experience by itself. This is an accurate mathematical analysis. I have been able to prove this. I can give you a mathematical statement as to how this happens. It always takes four.

5 P.M.
Tuesday
Jan 6, 1981

Any one of many five o'clock experiences: having tea at X; met several people; many rememberable environmental items.

| | |
|---|---|
| 5 P.M.<br>Tuesday<br>Feb 3, '81 | "It seems to me that this happened to me before." "Oh, now I remember, it must be coincidence." |
| 5 P.M.<br>Tuesday<br>March 3, '81 | "What again?" "How long ago was that? And the time before?" "If this is not strange coincidence, it will happen again on March 31st." |
| 5 P.M.<br>Tuesday<br>March 31, '81 | "Sure enough, I have discovered a periodic experience." |

It always takes a minimum of four equi-intervalled, identical, repeat-experiences to discover time dimensioning.

*Other relationships of four*

You may find many scientists going over what it is they have learned. One of the things they keep saying today is, "How does it happen? That it is always the number 4." This has a great deal to do with what I told you in yesterday's lecture when I spoke about Linus Pauling's Nobel Laureate review of the history of organic chemistry.

In 1880, a man named Frankland noted that in organic chemistry the numbers 1, 2, 3 and 4 were always being manifested. In 1825, a French chemist named Butlerev said that the 1, 2, 3 and 4 number repeatings related to the interbonding of chemical molecules. Butlerev called bonding "valence." He noted that there were uni-valent, bi-valent, tri-valent and quadri-valent organic chemical bondings.

In 1860, we have a chemist named Van't Hoff who stated that the recurrent oneness, twoness, threeness and fourness related to the four corners of the geometrical form, the tetrahedron.

*Tetrahedron as minimum structural system*

In my modern synergetic geometry I proved that the tetrahedron is the minimum structural system in the universe.

In my lecture last night, I reviewed the history of Van't Hoff's being rejected by science, which claimed that nature had no geometrical models, only mathematical equations. Van't Hoff lived to give optical proof of the tetrahedronal configuration of carbon. He was the first chemist ever to receive the Nobel prize.

DIL Dr. Fuller, will you please explain precisely what you mean by the term "system" and "structural system" in nature and the universe? It appears to be a central concept in your thinking and I would like to understand it more clearly.

FULLER Last night in my lecture I spoke to you about systems. I defined "system" to you. To elucidate on this thinking, I am borrowing a few pages from my in progress book, *Cosmography*.

*Meaning of*
*"structural system"*

Walk over a path or a roadway of recently-crushed stones. You will soon discover that no matter how many times stones are broken into smaller stones, none are ever produced with fewer than four corners, nor with fewer than three faces around each corner, nor with fewer than three edges around each face. You will also learn that frequently the recurrent form is that of an irregular tetrahedron. You are learning that nature has minute, mathematically elegant mini-terminal aspects.
Stones are always polyhedra — many sided. Even when stones appear to be polished spheroids, if looked at through a lens of sufficient magnifying power they will always be seen to be in fact many mini-mountained poly-poly-polyhedra.
The great eighteenth-century Swiss mathematician, Leonhard Euler, made an epochal breakthrough for mathematics and indirectly for all humanity when he discovered a set of always and only manifest unique patternings present in all our geometrical experiences. The patternings he named topology. He showed that all our visually-pictured experiences are always and only resolvable into three unique aspects: firstly *lines*, secondly *crossings* of lines (which can be called "fixes" or "vertices" or "points" or "corners") and thirdly *areas* (or faces) surrounded by the lines.

Euler showed that a universal law obtained which demonstrated that the number of *corners* (points, fixes, crossings, etc.) of all polyhedra plus the number of areas of the considered polyhedron will always equal the number of edges of that polyhedron plus two.

This formula is written as $V + F = E + 2$. To further elucidate Euler, I introduce my (not Euler's or anyone else's) SYSTEM concept.

A system is the simplest experience we can have. Systems always have insideness and outsideness. Recognition of a system begins either with the initial discovery of self or of the "otherness." Life begins with awareness. No "otherness," no awareness. No insideness and outsideness. No life or thought.

*Division of systems* Systems always divide all the universe into three principal parts. First, into the system itself. Second, into all the universe otherness outside the system — i.e., the macrocosm. And third, into all the system's microcosm — i.e., all the otherness inside the system.

More precisely, the foregoing three-way division can be expanded into five zones: First, into all the universe outside the system being considered, which in turn is divided into: (1) the clearly irrelevant macrocosm and, (2) the twilight macrocosm zone of "could-be-considered-relevant" external environment. Second, into the microcosmic insideness which in turn is divided into: (3) the clearly irrelevant microcosm and, (4) the twilight microcosm zone of "could-be-considered-as-relevant" in the internal environment of the microcosmic system and, (5) into the remaining portion of Universe which is the clearly relevant, clearly tuned-in system itself that convergently-divergently divides all the universe into its macro-outsideness and its micro-insideness irrelevancies.

*Thought systems* Systems have the powerful capability to spontaneously brain-employ our inward-outward, convergent-divergent, concave-convex, sorting-out differentiating. All

65

thoughts also are always spontaneous tunings-in of uniquely inter-relevant thought systems.

Thought systems consist of all the clearly-relevant considerations. Consideration (con-sidus) means literally bringing together and being concerned with the spontaneously-discovered interrelatedness of a special star group — that is to say, with special constellation of neighboring star thoughts.

Thought systems have their spontaneously-conceived macro- and micro-relevant limits. There are events too large and too infrequent to be spontaneously considered and events too small and/or of too high a frequency to be noticeably tune-in-able within our magnitude of macro-micro range considerations.

Thoughts, as with TV programs, have their "tuned-in," always discrete, special wavelengths and frequencies. These tuned-in frequencies inherently exclude all the multitude of neighboring, untuned-in macro- and micro-frequencies of concurrently broadcast programs. The tuned-in TV programs unfortunately include irrelevantly-intruded advertising, which trespasses upon not only our chosen programs, but upon a major number of awake hours of our entire lifetime.

Universe is ever intensively — intertensionally — pulsing and resonating, convergently-divergently, explosively, implosively in a vast range of system frequencies, magnitudes and chords. If our corporeal organism has the normal human equipment, it may be in-tensionally intensively tuned-in. We may become intertuned with other individual, special-case human systems.

By Bucky Fuller's "system law," all systems are always polyhedronal and by Euler's law all polyhedra only consist of corners, faces and edges. There is, therefore, a topologically-systemic program of thinking. The thinking operation may be systemically programmed into a computer. The computer may be systemically programmed to reject any topological discrepancies. It can give you answers only to specific system questions. It cannot answer a "What shall I do?" It can answer: "Which is the most physically advantageous way — this way or that way?" after you have programmed the computer with all the relevant data leading to each of the system's two possible answers.

Take note of the fact that the Greeks mistakenly assumed that a phenomenon "solid" existed. In respect to the most prominently-remembered Greeks, all but Democritus assumed marble to be "solid." We now know by instrumentally-evidenced experience that the electron is as remote from its nucleus as is the Earth from the Moon, as compared in the diameters of their respective spheric-domains of activities. We now know there are no "solids." Thinking of solids as realistic caused the Greeks to think of Plato's carved-out cubes, octahedra, tetrahedra, icosahedra, and dodecahedra's *faces, sides,* or *areas bound* within the edge lines of those "solids" as being very "obviously" existent *faces* or *sides* or "hedra." Ergo all multi-faceted solid geometry objects became known as polyhedra and are as yet so thought of.

*Nonexistence of solids*

We hope our comprehensively-inclusive review of the facts may alter the educational continuance of such errors.

Because we now know that no solids exist — there are no solid sides or faces — we must now identify the geometric systems as "Polyvertexia" instead of "Polyhedra."

Sir James Jeans pronounced what is to me the most sensitively-inclusive and accurate definition of "science" when he said, "Science is the sincere and consistent attempt to set in order the facts of experience." Ernst Mach, the Viennese physicist whose name is associated with the unit of supersonic speed — "Mach number" — spontaneously and specifically elaborated on Jeans' generalization when Mach said, "Physics is the attempt to set the facts of ex-

*Jeans' definition of science*

perience in the *most economical order*." Jeans' comprehensive "science" considered any order such as relative size or color or weight. Mach's physics had found that nature always accomplished her tasks in the most economical energy-employing and -expending manner. Ergo his *special case of science* definition of *physics* as seeking to set in most energy-efficient (economic) order the facts of experience.

*Recording of Euler's topological characteristics*

Since I am intent upon comprehending what experiences are trying to communicate scientifically to us, and since I am intent upon being consistently scientific, I have in my sorting out of facts and rearranging them in systemic order of relevancy to reword Euler's topological characteristics. Since what I have learned is that all experiences are systems, and that systems can be and often are microtuneable to non-differentiable wavelengths and frequencies, and that sub-micro-tuneable-limit cases of electromagnetic "signals" are known as "static." I will now identify the micro-fixes as "static" events (corners, vertexes, etc.) and I will identify the micro-minimum system as "somethings." I will also reidentify the system "facets" as window-framed views of nothingness to be symbolized as △ or, as is the symbol O — the cipher, the circular window of nothingness. And I will identify the six most economical lines of interrelatedness of the four "static" *somethings* defining the four corners of the minimum system embracingly defining the *tetravertexion* as the minimally and always six-part convergent minimum-set of push-pull energy vectors structurally integrating the tetravertexion — the minimum structural system of Universe.

Euler's equation now reads the number of somethings plus the number of framed views of nothingness will always equal the number of lines of interrelationships of the number of somethings plus the number two.

There is no identifiable experience which is less than a system. Two events have only betweenness. Three events have only betweenness. Not until we have four corner events do we have insideness and outsideness differentiating guide points. To inclusively differentiate and identify insideness and outsideness takes a minimum of four micro-wavelength and -frequency "static electricity" locuses to includingly define a tune-in-able wavelength and frequency system.

The minimum system is the tetravertexion which consists of four corners (vertices) plus four triangular window-framed views of four congruent internal nothingnesses and six lines of interrelatedness of the four-corner somethings.

Thus, progressively considered, Euler's equation now reads the number of something corners plus the number of interrelationship-framed views of nothingnesses always equals the number of linear interrelationships of the system plus the number two.

Since the most unique aspect of a system is its cosmic independence of existence, and since all independent systems have independent rotatability, they all have uniquely-identifiable axes of spinnability or all-around overall viewability.

Axes of spinnability always have two poles. We may now most economically restate Euler's topological formula of constant interrelative abundance of primitive aspects of all systems as follows: in all polyvertexia, the two vertexially-operative poles of axial spin plus the number of nonpolar vertexia plus the number of lines of interrelationship-framed window views of internal nothingnesses will always equal the total number of uniquely-most-economical, vectorial, linear interrelationships of the system's corner vertexia "somethings."

I never employ axioms meaning "it is evident" or "it has always been assumed to be true that." I am a scientific

69

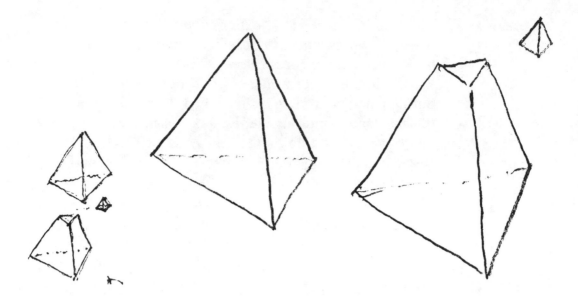

mathematician since my raw material is always experimentally-redemonstratable, physical evidence. The product of that experimentally-based science is the following table of cosmically-primitive hierarchy of nature's structuring systems and their constant-interrelationship volumetric and topological values.

*Mathematical law
eternally constant*

If I knock off one corner from any one of the regular-symmetrical polyvertexia, making it irregular, the law persists. Mathematical law is eternally, infinitely constant. For instance, if we knock off one corner of the tetravertextion we leave in its place a small triangular facet. We have now lost one old corner and gained three new corners (net gain: two corners) and gained one additional face and three additional new edges. The total score is now $6 + 5 = 9 + 2$ (i.e. six corners plus five faces equals nine edges plus two).

It doesn't matter if our original tetrahedron or octahedron or icosahedron or thought, or stone, is irregular in its angular, linear or facial dimensions.

Euler had discovered that his topology embraced all viewable features of any system. If it is a Rembrandt or a child's freely-ranging (so-called two-dimensional) pencil drawing you will find that the whole picture scheme always can be sorted into lines (edges), areas (faces), and crossings (corner points or vertices) without any left-over features of the picture.

In fact, a sheet of paper is always a very thin polyhedron of two large, front and back faces and four very narrow side faces and eight corners and twelve edges.

The points, lines, areas may be of any color — where a colored area creases a line occurs. No matter how you choose to classify any feature of a Rembrandt, the relative abundance of lines, points and areas the formula will hold.

*Function of brain versus mind* I have mentioned before my differentiation between "brain" and "mind." Brains are physical atoms and molecules, operating entirely inside the physical skull. Brains are always and only coordinating the information that is being fed in from outside the skull by the senses — smelling, touching, hearing and seeing. The information is always a special case. "This one smells a little differently from that." Brains are always and only dealing, then, with temporal, terminal, special-case experiences.

Minds are entirely metaphysical. Minds, from time to time, discover relationships existing between special cases that cannot be smelled, touched, seen or heard. Such, for instance, is Kepler's, Galileo's, and Newton's combined discovery of the mass interattraction of celestial bodies, i.e., gravity, which could only be inversely expressed as a second power of the arithmetical distances intervening. Halve the distance and the interattraction increases fourfold.

71

You can't see, smell, touch or hear the mass interattraction intercohering either the macro-or micro-bodies of the universe. Such interrelationships can be discovered only by the mind.

Mind seems to be universal. It can be tuned into the individual who is intent upon finding the true interrelationships of our experiences.

*First four numbers*

It is pure metaphysical speculation, but extremely interesting to note, that the names for the first four numbers 1, 2, 3, 4 in many languages are often used in songs: "Eins, zwei, drei, vier"; "ichi, ni, san, shi", which names for words are very different from the names of all the other names for numbers. In the chapter on numerology in my book *Synergetics*[24] I show how the numbers 1, 2, 3, and 4 have additive effects on other numbers and the numbers 5, 6, 7, and 8 have subtractive effects and how the number 9 has a neutral effect. I demonstrate the positive-negative tetravertexioning of successive octaves consisting always of the positive-negative half octaves formed by the succession of positive-negative tetrahedra. It is notable that only the tetrahedron can turn itself inside-out. The tetrahedron is apparently the "black hole" turned out of physical state phenomena.

One, two, three, four
Sometimes I wish
There were more.

Eins, zwei, drei, vier
I love the one
That's near

Ichi, ni, san, shi . . .

From Harvard Glee Club Song 1900
(Origin unknown)

DIL                    What would you say is the commonality in the way Leo-
                       nardo da Vinci, Albert Einstein, Buckminster Fuller and
                       such people think? What would you then say is the com-
                       mon pattern, if it were possible to describe it very briefly?

FULLER                 I wrote a book called *Intuition,* and intuition is the es-
                       sence. In my book I reviewed how the word intuition be-
*Intuition common*     came almost a "dirty word" in the 1920s world of science
*to great scientists*  and technology.
                       I would like to return to consideration of Einstein's cos-
                       mic religious sense essay, published in the *New York
                       Times Magazine* in 1930, when the USSR atheism was
                       spreading amongst the western world's intellectuals who
                       were assuming that the 1929 crash and its abysmal reces-
                       sion phase in 1930 meant that capitalism was dead. Ein-
                       stein's cosmic religious sense is inherently intuitive.
                       In the USSR's 1920s ideological war strategy, the word
                       *intuition* was too dangerously mystical to be tolerated by
                       an atheistic pragmatism. For a protracted period during
                       the Great Depression, there was a general, western-
                       world, intellectual, university-supported forsaking of ac-
                       creditation of the concept and the word *intuition* and oth-
                       er metaphysical-phenomena words. To the new commu-
                       nist pragmatists in the United States, science did not use
                       intuition; it simply stated its problems and solved them by
                       empirical means.

I myself have always held that my intuition is the most important faculty that I have.

I was very pleased when in the 1950s F. S. C. Northrop at Yale and a professor at another university, quite unbeknownst to one another, made a search of the personal papers of three great scientists who all the world agreed had made great physical knowledge discoveries on behalf of all humanity. What Northrop and his independent-researcher counterpart examined were the personal letters, personal scientific notes, and the scientist's immediate family's and immediate friends' letters as written only just before and slightly after the great scientists made their great discoveries.

*First intuition*

Both research professors found that all these three great scientists, who existed far apart in years and geography, made it perfectly clear in their written record that the single most important factor in their great discoveries was their intuition. The sudden strange impulse to look in this or that particular direction when you are physically busy over here led to making their great discoveries.

*Second intuition*

The second most important factor was a second intuition that occurred soon after they had made their great discoveries. The second intuition was always the awareness of what needed to be done "right now" if they wished to safely secure the great discovery they had just made as a practically-realizable physical advantage for humanity. The second intuition might tell them, for instance, not to smoke another cigarette, not to go out to lunch, but to sit down right now and produce a clear documentation of the discovery. This first and second intuition is analogous to a fisherman, alerted by the nibbling on baited hook and sinker, realizing that he must jerk his line to secure the hooking and then must pull the line in and land the fish. All this first and second intuitioning was clear in the notes of these great discoverers. This published and widely-read information of Professor Northrop powerfully re-accredited the intuition function amongst the scientific intellectuals. To proliferate this knowledge I wrote my book *Intuition*. In it I find intuition and aesthetics to be two vitally important faculties of humans' brains and minds.

*Aesthetics*

Humans usually learn of the word *aesthetics* after their childhood. It is, however, pure aesthetics that makes a child love the sight of this or that. I think that I had personally very great good fortune in that my eyes at birth were and still are deformed to a significant degree. I do not know what went on when I was in my mother's womb. At any rate, my eyes are misshapen. All that I have to do today is take off my glasses if I wish to see what I saw until I was four-and-a-half years old. I have the same basic corrective lenses of my first 1899 prescription. Magnification has been added as I grow older. Without my glasses I cannot see anything as detailed as human eyes. For my first four-and-a-half years, I did not have glasses. All I could see were colors, brightness, shadows, darkness and outlines of large objects. As I take off my glasses now, all I can see is color. I was extremely sensitive to color. I was extremely sensitive to smells. I was extremely sensitive to touching. Not having the power of the eyes, which is so much greater than our other three faculties, imagine my astonishment when they gave me glasses to suddenly see eyes. I became so excited. I found that frogs had eyes, and toads had eyes, and snakes had eyes, and I kept looking deeply and intently into their eyes. They did the same to me. We seemed to say to each other, "I love and trust you."

*Fuller's eyesight problem*

So I went through the "second take" of life. It was like a rebirth. It gave me two kinds of ways of looking at things and therefore two different ways of thinking about my experiences: in the hazy color way and in the detailed way.

I kept looking at human eyes and also snakes' eyes and I found that the snake and I could talk to each other. As a child I would say intuitively that I have got to take this snake home because I love him. When my family or nurse began to take off my clothes, they would shriek because my clothes were full of snakes. I became very sensitive to what other people felt about different beautiful things. So, aesthetics to me was the live functioning of a flower, the ephemeral existence of a drop of water, and of the dew of the lilies. Fortunately, my childhood home had a lovely garden.

DIL     Intuition and aesthetic sensibility then, in your view, comprise a commonality among Leonardo da Vinci, Albert Einstein, and Buckminster Fuller. I am interested in seeing how such people think. How does the thinking process take shape in the mind? So that if every human child is born with the potential to be a genius, as you say, and to function at a certain level of excellence, to look at life with wonder, to enjoy life, to have so much fun in living, then why is there so much wastage taking place in human life? I am not talking only of great achievements, but of experiencing everyday joys: for example, the joy of drinking a cup of water and having full enjoyment of such common experiences of life once one has become aware of their function and significance in life. Because if this does not happen to the average human being, life won't be enhanced, and we are going to be living at a limited and lower level of humanity. The limits of human life must be extended and enriched in everyday common living. As I see it, this is what you are trying to do through your explorations as you report them in your world-embracing lectures and publications.

FULLER     In exploring *intuition* and *aesthetics*, I've discovered something about how each one works.

Number one, we all have the experience of discovering and saying, "What is the name of that mutual friend of ours; I can't quite remember it." Then the next morning I'll remember it. You've had the same experience. So we all have the experience of asking ourselves a question that gets answered by ourselves later on. In other words, this tells us we have a reliable subconscious functioning operative in our brains even while we sleep. Let's try to identify it.

Nowadays I'm traveling ninety percent of the time. With my very poor hearing sometimes I don't have the ability to hear the telephone or the alarm clock ringing. But I am also often very tired; I swiftly reckon that I could sleep for perhaps three-and-a-quarter hours and then be awakened by that same subconscious faculty activity that retrieved the forgotten name for me while I slept. I intuitively dare do that if there is nobody, nor an adequate mechanical alarm, to wake me up. So what I do is to think up experiences I've had that are about three-hours-and-a-quarter long. Then I lie down and I wake up exactly three-hours-and-a-quarter later, right to the minute. This unconscious organization that goes on is employable by us willfully if we do some thinking about various magnitudes of time. I'm astonished to find I can wake myself in exactly three hours and fifty-seven minutes if I want to. I've got to do a little thinking first to be sure I remember an experience that was exactly three hours and fifty-seven minutes long, but it will work right to the minute. So what I have established now is that we have a subconscious monitoring process going on in our brain that employs experiences of various magnitudes, which can be reemployed. Once I have established that we have a subconscious monitoring system, I then make another experiment. This has to do with our "twilight zone" consciousness.

I stretch both my arms forward and parallel to each other. I turn my two index fingers skyward. I now swing my outstretched arms horizontally away from one another with index fingers as yet skyward-stretched. I keep looking straight ahead but realize that while looking straight ahead I can also see both of my skyward-pointed index fingers. I can see them clearly even when my arms are stretched out sideways, though I say to myself that I am looking straight ahead.

This experiment tells us that there are many events taking place in our lives at which we are not consciously looking but of which we are semiconsciously aware. It is this semiconsciousness which at times arouses our intuition to look directly in this and that direction and thereby discover some sensorially-apprehendible phenomena of significant relevance to our system's thinking. Semisubconscious awareness of our experience often constitutes the fourth event which produces the significant system-embracing event which produces comprehension of all the system's interrelationships and even its relationships to other significant systems. Semisubconscious awareness relates to a very effective and available basis for becoming aware of what is going on, in looking this way and looking that way.

I think the intuition relates to what I have said earlier about recognizing the significance of the "third" experience — that this is the third experience in which I felt intuitively that I've felt it before. The difference between the Leonardo da Vincis, Albert Einsteins and other people is that the other people don't pay attention to the third experience in the series of four system-defining events. The Leonardos and Einsteins pay powerful attention to the third event.

When I was very young on our island in Maine, my father and mother gave me a sailboat when I could first swim. It was a very nice little sailing dinghy. One day my father and mother and a girl cousin took my boat and went off from the island and sailed out of sight. They were going to another island several miles away to get our island's mail. All of a sudden I became terrifiedly aware that something had happened to them. It was true, a storm had come up and it was a bad day, and with my experience of sailing the boat, I had become sensitive to the fact that these were pretty bad conditions to cope with. It was raining when they took off and they had worn their storm oilskins. They had wanted to get the mail. It was very important mail. I ran from our island's harbor to the older people of the family at the other end of the island. I was then nine. I was frighteningly certain that my father, mother and cousin were in trouble. Because I was so young, the rest of the family was not impressed. One of my cousins had married a minister, and he finally decided that they had best listen to Bucky. He decided to do something about it. He went down with me to our half-mile-away island harbor and got our captain who was a native fisherman-farmer. He sailed our big thirty-five-foot auxiliary-engined Friendship sloop. We sent him off with the big boat, and sure enough, he found my parents and cousin had been capsized and luckily had been able to swim to a nearby island. They were perishing with cold. The captain brought them home with my dinghy in tow.

That experience in my childhood made me absolutely certain of my clairvoyantly-valid awareness that they were in peril. I think it happens to many, many children. That must be built on all kinds of other things such as when you are in the womb and things are happening to *Different kinds of* your mother outside there, and you are aware of it. What *awareness* kinds of awareness of things do transpire while we are in the womb? Are you aware of something outside? Probably, but not in geometrically-conceptual terms since you have never yet seen anything.

79

I keep speculating on what, if anything, subconsciousness does while we are as yet in the womb. A newborn baby whose eyes are not yet open moves its fingers deftly. If you put your finger in its hand, the fingers close firmly on your finger. If you decide to move your finger away, the newborn baby's fingers immediately open. There is a real communication of touch already established at birth. What happens to unwanted babies while they are in the womb?

We now know that all human beings have an electromagnetic field of incredibly high frequency and low voltage. It is very difficult to read, but it is there. And when we are feeling negative, it produces a negative field, and when we are feeling positive, it produces a positive field. This may be why people drink together — to release the positive "good-fellowship field" among them. Thus far we don't know very much about these ultra, ultra shortwave phenomena. Mainly I'm trying to give my concepts about aesthetics and intuition. They are probably all interrelated.

*The aesthetic sense and biological structuring*

In the matter of aesthetics, our sense of smell, of healthy growth (which is the smell of a new baby), and fresh biscuits, gives a smelling sense of growth versus decay. This also has something to do with our sense of balance and our spontaneous gauge of accuracy in design. Our sense of convergence and divergence most augment our growth and decay appraising. I think that the great sculptors of the era of the great sculpture in Greece and Italy had an incredible aesthetic sense of structure and function, of functional adequacy and of proportion as manifest, for example, in their drawing the neck or back of a woman. I see that this judgment of good design and accuracy often comes while looking at flowers, petals and stems. Our sense of shape or of compound curvature is keen. In biological structuring, the compressional function is accomplished by hydraulics. The crystalline intertensioning contains the compressional hydraulic stresses. Liquids distribute their loads. Crystalline will not distribute a load but liquids do. Liquids are noncompressible. Gases are compressible. Liquids are flexible but noncompressible. Liquids, then, guarantee the firmness of all biological, botanical and zoological structuring.

All human beings are over sixty percent water. We have crystalline tensional sacks filled with liquid. The sacks overlap each other like fibers spun into thread. The liquid-filled sacks are often held together by spiraling-crystal intertensioning. We have a great sense of how much liquids are coming in or out of our system. We have structural-understanding propensities.

*Structural integrity of triangles*

We feel the structural integrity of triangles. If we make a large necklace with four or more, six-inch long aluminum tubes strung together on dacron line, we will find it very flexible, which means structurally unstable.

We find that the flexing is done by the short lengths of dacron cord running between the tubes' ends. Hoping to isolate the flexing phenomenon, we keep taking tubes out of our necklace. Then we get to only five, then four tubes being left in the necklace; it is as yet completely flexible. We now oust one more tube and that is the last we can take out and have the assembly produce a necklace having an opening through it.

The Greeks used the name "polygon" for planar-pattern geometrical figures. Six tubes left in the necklace lying on a table produce a hexagon ("gon" means side), five tubes make a pentagon, four tubes a square, and the three final tubes left in the configuration produce a triangle. It is the first and only polygon to hold its shape. It is also the minimum, terminal case of a polygon series.

*Definitions of structure and system*

The triangle, which holds its shape despite flexible corners, is structure. I define structure as a complex of events that interact to produce a stable pattern. I define a system as that which has an insideness and an outside-

81

ness. There are only three structural, omni-equi-angle triangle-enclosed systems in Universe — the four-vertex, six-vertex, and twelve-vertex systems. In Old Greek, they are called the tetrahedron, octahedron, and icosahedron. Altogether, all crystals and all biological design are made up from those three. When we fasten three corners of a triangular face of any one of the three prime structural systems of Universe together, they form a rigid crystal. When we bring two corners of each of the prime structural systems together, they form a hinge and produce a liquid behavior that can articulate and distribute stresses, but never compress. If we bring one corner of each of two of our prime structural systems together, they will bind to one another in an open stress-distributing but compressible system as a gas.

"It is possible to identify some of the known faculties which we generally assume to be coordinate in those whom society does concede to be adult geniuses. The publicly-accredited characteristics of genius consist for instance of an actively self-attended *intuition* opening the conceptual doors for *innate, frequently and combiningly employed, scientific, artistic, philosophical, idealistic, sensorily conceptive, physically talented, logical, farsighted, imaginative* and *practical* articulations.

Leonardo da Vinci, who fortunately avoided the genius-eroding processes, manifested and coordinatingly employed all and more of such conceptual faculties and articulative capabilities."

— Buckminster Fuller in his discourse as the
Third Jawaharlal Nehru Memorial Lecturer,
New Delhi, 1969.

*Leonardo da Vinci. Self-Portrait. c. 1512–15. Red chalk. $13^1/_8 \times 8^3/_8''$.*
*Royal Library, Turin.*

I think aesthetics is built on an innate sense of the stress distribution, flexing, and rigidifying capabilities. I am the first to show why these system interbondings are single-bondedly the gases, double-bondedly are the liquids, and triple-bondedly are the crystallines. We have a universe-outside (macro-) and a universe-inside (micro-) set of systems interbonded to produce all physical matter. Our thoughts, our experiences, the book, the table — all are systems.

I say life begins with awareness, and with no otherness there is no awareness. Life begins when you get outside — come out of the insideness of the womb and become both insideness and outsideness and self-observing — and realize the outsideness and insideness of the otherness. Our innate genius led me to discover a system and the structural mathematics of systems. This system, which I call synergetics, is now beginning to be recognized and is upsetting all academic mathematics and science. I have enough confidence in my experiences to dare to rely on my natural intuitions and my natural aesthetics and feelings, which led me to making experiments and thereby acquiring experimental evidence of the heretofore-only-intuitively-dreamed-to-be-possible structuring.

Intuitions often turn dreams into demonstrable facts.

One thing that really inspires so much hope in me is that people like Leonardo da Vinci, Albert Einstein, and Buckminster Fuller are so full of hope, as contrasted with people like Bertrand Russell who are, in general, skeptical and pessimistic. I hope I am not being unfair to Russell. I have great admiration for his intellect, but at the same time there is a certain lack of hopefulness, almost despair, in his view of human future; for example, in his 1950 essay "The Future of Mankind" and the 1961 book *Has Man a Future*.[25]

What is it that gives you so much hope? You are one of the most optimistic and hope-inspiring scientist-philosophers of our time, and your writings are full of promise for the future of humankind. The same can be said of Albert Einstein, even though especially in later life his mind was burdened by the problems of the misuse of nuclear energy, and a number of other complex issues of our time. Leonardo was faced with complex problems of both personal and social nature that might have crushed a lesser person. You have experienced critical problems in your own life and continuously write and speak about a number of them. For example, in your lecture last evening you presented a forceful discussion of the increasing threat of atomic holocaust by the more than 50,000 poised-for-delivery atomic bombs. And your newest book, *Grunch of Giants*,[26] is an eye-opening discussion of the power of the military-industrial complex that has led to the emergence of the powerful and mighty multinational corporations that control the economic and political future of humankind. How do you keep the light of hope alive?

FULLER

Because in contrast to the specialists of science and technology, I am a comprehensive thinker and doer. I am also a sailor, a navigator with unlimited first-class maritime papers. I am a licensed airplane pilot. I am a card-carrying member of the oldest labor union in the United States, the International Association of Machinists and Aerospace Workers. I am committed to solving problems with technology and not with politics. I am apolitical.

Over 300,000 of the geodesic domes which I have invented are now operational all around the world, from the point in Greenland closest to the North Pole to one exactly over the South Pole of our planet. One hundred thousand of the geodesic domes are in city playgrounds around the world, teaching children how best to enclose space. I set about fifty-five years ago to take advantage of the invisible evolution in chemistry, metallurgy, electronics and mass-production techniques, wherein we continually achieve ever-more-advanced standards of product and service performance per each pound of material and erg of energy and second of time invested in the technological undertaking.

I found in 1917 that all world-dominant political, economic, religious and business-organization economics were formalized when the British Empire was established in 1805, with their winning of Trafalgar and control thereby of all the important sea lanes of the planet. The British Empire was historically the first empire on which it was said that "the sun never set." It embodied a closed-system planet in contradistinction to the misassumed lateral extension in all directions to infinity of the Roman Empire. Thomas Malthus, professor of political economics at the East India College, near London, was the first human in history to have all the vital statistics and comprehensive resource inventory of the closed-system earth. All world economics are predicated on the 1803 Malthusian conclusion that there is a major and fundamental inadequacy of life support on our planet which, combined with Darwin's fifty-six-year-later evolutionary law of "survival of the fittest" governs all world political, religious and business organizations.

My theory on how to cope with the seeming inadequacy of life support was to employ, multiply and accelerate the invisible technology gains to such a degree as to take care of all the people — gains such as that of a one-and-three-quarter-ton communications satellite outperforming in performance fidelity and message capacity the trans-oceanic communications capability of 375 thousand tons of copper cable.

*The first geodesic domes*

When I produced my first geodesic domes, the two largest domes in the world were in Rome. Both were 150 feet in diameter: St. Peter's Dome, built circa A. D. 1000 and the Pantheon, built in the year A. D. 1. Each of those old domes weighed about thirty thousand tons. My first 150-foot geodesic dome weighed thirty tons, only one-thousandth of conventional masonry domes. My dome was earthquake-proof, and the two Roman masonry domes were not. I have not only been developing unlimited-clear-span geodesic domes but also have been keeping track for fifty-five years of all the performance gains in chemistry, metallurgy, and electronics.

In structures there always exist compression and tension. They always and only coexist, as do concave and convex. Radiation is the divergent compressive force of Universe and gravity is Universe's convergent tensional force.

*Structural materials and the design revolution*

Masonry has a compression-resisting force of 50,000 pounds per square inch but masonry has a tension capability of only fifty pounds per square inch. The best and most plentiful wood has a tensile strength of 10,000 pounds per square inch.

In 1851, production steel was inaugurated. Like masonry, it had a compressive strength of 50,000 pounds per square inch (p.s.i.). But unlike masonry, it had also a tensile strength of 50,000 p.s.i., five times that of wood. Since then, in 1883, carbon steel went to 70,000 p.s.i. In World War I, chrome-molybdenum steel went to 110,000 p.s.i. In World War II, chrome-nickel steel

87

brought tensional capability to 350,000 p.s.i. with never an increase in weight or volume. And now, at the onset of the 1980s, we have come to practical use of epoxy-bonded-together carbon fibers with 600,000 p.s.i. plus, and a great reduction of weight per pound as compared with aluminum or steel. McCready's ninety-five-foot-wing-span, trans-English-Channel, human-peddling-flown "gossamer albatross," made of epoxy-bonded carbon fibers and mylar skin, weighed only forty-five pounds. Anyone could lift it with one hand.

In 1970, world-around technology had advanced so greatly in performance per each pound of material, erg of energy and second of time invested per each accomplished unit of performance, that it could be clearly demonstrated by engineering that operating on a world-around design science revolution and using all the metals now invested in armaments, melting them down and reinvesting them in livingry, we could within ten years have all humanity living at a sustainable higher standard of living than ever experienced by any other human, while concurrently phasing out all further use of fossil fuels and atomic energy. No cheers nor offers of realization came from the oil companies.

The reason you find me hope-giving is that I have discovered humanity's option to "make it," which option was heretofore unknown to exist. War is now obsolete. It does not have to be you or me. I know what I am talking about and that gives you confidence.

*Humanity learns by trial and error* Because advertising pays for newspaper publishing and is placed with the journals that are most popularly read, publishers have sought to feed out what kind of news sells the most. They have found that *bad news* sells best. Humanity designed to be born naked, helpless and ignorant yet endowed with hunger, thirst and curiosity is forced to learn only by trial and error. Bad news is what steers humanity. Writers are paid most for being brilliantly negative, and develop a popular vocabulary to be brilliantly negative. Many do that to make a living. To be positive, you have to know what you're talking about, and I do. Most writers are ignorant of the significance of the 99.999 percent invisible technology.

Realizing the parts which the brain cannot comprehend, in themselves — the brain cannot do the thinking — so my confidence is in the human mind, which has access to the great principles of the universe itself, to find those cosmic laws.

I think I was very fortunate in my schooling to have a very extraordinary physics teacher who gave me enormous confidence in organizing experiments to find out

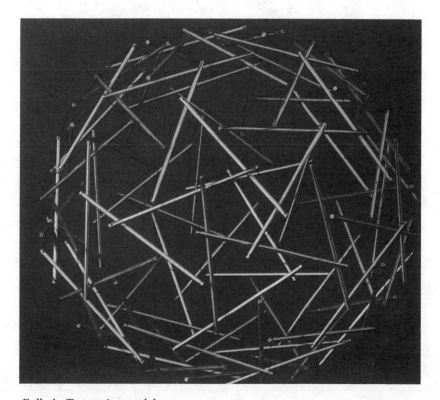

*Fuller's Tensegrity model*

how principles work: how light comes through little holes; discovering that there are mathematical angles and ratios involved; learning how to check my work. In my life I have been able to find and discover generalized principles of structure, that I've been able to discover how Universe is structured without anything touching anything else. In discovering and producing my exclusively *tensional* integrity structural systems (i. e., tensegrities), I am only finding out how to use on our planet Earth what Kepler found to be going on in the heavens around us. I reduced it to practice. This proved that I was very lucky that when I first started getting into trouble at Harvard, I went off and became a mechanic and learned how to assemble each and every type of cotton-mill machinery. I learned about machine shops, foundries and forging.

*Discovering tensegrity*

I was very lucky to have been a sailor, very lucky that my family lived on an island where as a boy I had to use a boat to get from here to there, and I had to get the mail every day and row four miles every day, to learn how to use the wind, how to navigate in the fog, how to fell and dress-out my own masts.

*Fuller's practical experiences*

I was very lucky to be a mechanic because my forebears had been ministers and lawyers with little physical experience, and I had much more physical experience than Einstein. I learned by building buildings.

Between 1922 and 1927, I built two hundred and forty buildings. I learned that people were building them the wrong way and what they were doing that was wrong. I had learned how you build and rig a ship. How you build a ship is very different from the way you build a house. I was very lucky in having to work in all twenty-eight Greater New York City branch sales houses of a large national meat-packing company, going to work at 3 A.M. and learning how New York City received its foods and how the markets operated.

I was lucky in my Navy experiences of World War I, having many types of experience in aircraft, radio and in commanding ships.

I was very, very lucky in having my physical experiences, which I think have given me many more insights regarding the physical significance of aesthetic beauty of line and tension. I have a structural-system subconsciousness.

*Young Fuller saves his boat*

One day when I was about fourteen and was sailing home with the mail to Bear Island on a dying northerly wind, I anchored my boat on the south side of our island because I knew my mother wanted me to get home for lunch. We had a good harbor on the north side. But after lunch the wind switched dramatically and as I came on to the high bluff above the shore, I saw that my boat was dragging its anchor, and its wooden stern transom was just beginning to be chewed on the rocks. I must have flown down to those rocks and in almost no time at all was holding my boat off, thinking, what can I do, the anchor is dragging, I can't really count on it, and the sail is not up, and my boat, if I let go for one second, is going to chew up on the rocks and get a hole and sink. So I began suddenly to use my mind and all my experiences. I could see an oar in the cockpit down under the gunwale, I could see everything inside the boat. I figured that though the anchor was dragging, that it had a little bit of holding capability. I then figured out what moment in the rising and falling of the boat I was holding off the rocks would be most propitious for me to jump aboard to grab the oar to thrust against the rock and hold us off from it. I figured out very rapidly how I could scull the boat out against the waves far enough to first take in the slack in the anchor rope, then to scull out some more into deeper water and next to get my sails on and give me time to beat off shore. I figured it all out and rehearsed it in my mind. I had no time to be discouraged. I did get on board, and with a number

91

of successive scullings between other functions I did get my boat off shore without any additional chewing of my stern by the rocks.

*Getting out of tailspins*

I am an air pilot and suddenly something goes wrong. I'm in a stall and now a tailspin. What do I do? There's a moment of being stunned by the fact, then a moment of absolute clarity in which you realize clearly that if in one fraction of a second you do this and that exactly right, you will pull out of your tailspin. Many times I've done these exact things in split seconds and have lived to so report. The fact is that I did find that I could get out of tailspins and get back to straight and level flight. It is also a fact that evolution has been constantly proving that I was really right when in 1927 I saw that there was comprehensive physical success for all humanity inherent in alloys, and inherent in the invisible technology of progressively attaining more and more performance with ever less and less pounds of material, ergs of energy and seconds of time per each accomplished function.

*Technology ground for hope*

I undertook to do those things, and they worked. So I am tremendously aware that it is highly feasible now to take care of all humanity and do so within a decade because we have the technology to do it. On the other hand, I find almost all intellectual, financial and political leaders technologically ignorant. They write very negatively, and I've found people who say that the technology is hell. They don't understand the most eternal physical fact which is that the physical universe is nothing but technology.

*Negative voices being silenced*

For reasons already given, there's been a great financial support of writers who are negative masters. I found myself up against that world, and I learned that I'm not God, and that God takes time for these things to correct themselves. However, I find it really fascinating and gratifying that most of the prominent and widely-listened-to negative voices that I was up against yesterday are being silenced. The young people aren't listening to them anymore.

*God as a positive factor*   But your question was, "Why am I so hopeful?" Because, as already reviewed, I have experienced making things work technologically. I find that evolution is trying to do so. Everything in evolution tells me that God is trying to make humans a success. That's why I'm hopeful. We have God on our side.

DIL   Well, is it possible that in the case of Bertrand Russell, who also knew science and technology, the main difference between you and him is that he did not believe in God? Is that perhaps one of the reasons for his skepticism?

FULLER   Yes, you bet!

DIL   How strongly do you feel about it?

FULLER   I feel very, very strongly. Russell knew a great deal about mathematics but not enough to discover synergetics. He knew very little of technology. He was declaredly committed to exclusively-political solutions of problems. He espoused communist atheism.

DIL
*Einstein's view of religion*   Einstein's concept of a religiously-inspired person was of one who has faith in God and has achieved freedom from the shackles of personal desires and fears. One of the highest goals of religion, to him, was to liberate mankind from the bondage of individual egocentric preoccupations. He believed that science could contribute to such cosmic spiritualization of human life. In his 1941 essay on science and religion,[27] he said that the path to genuine religiousness does not lie through the fear of life and death, and it cannot be reached through blind faith but through rational knowledge, thereby acquiring that profound reverence which is the essence of true religiousness.

93

He had the cosmic religious sense. Einstein said what a faith in the orderliness of Universe must have inspired Kepler, to be able to spend all the nights of his life alone with the stars, lonely, alone, alone. "Belief" is what others tell you. "Faith" is in the significance of that which you yourself have witnessed.

I have absolute faith in what I call the intellectual integrity of the eternally-regenerative universe and in its integrated, only mathematically-stateable eternal principles.

Fifty-five years ago, at the age of thirty-two, I undertook experiments to see what the little penniless, unaccredited, unknown human being might be able to do effectively on behalf of all humanity that it was inherently impossible for political states, private enterprise and all religious organizations to do. I decided to commit myself to doing everything with artifacts and not with politics and not trying to reform humans. I knew that I was going to need tools, expensive materials. I knew I was going to have to make prototypes, not just talk about them. I knew that just talking about an invention is useless. Inventions must be reduced to working size, physical practice if I was to prove that it would work and that it would indeed do more with less. Obviously those materials and tools were going to cost a lot of money. And nobody with money, public or private, was interested in backing me. So I said, "I am going to have to assume that these very expensive things I am undertaking to do, not to make money but in order to help make humanity a physical success, are apparently what God wants us to do." Remember, I called God the intellectual integrity of the universe. I may find I'll get on because I see that the grass doesn't have to pay the clouds for the rain, the earth doesn't have to pay the sun for the radiation. Money is not involved in any of nature's intertransforming transactions. Money is an invention of man and is not a requirement of Universe. As a man, I'll be doing what the universe wants done, I'll be part of evolution, employing a capability that has been put into humans to employ. This is the time when we have the knowledge and words and tools to make humans physically successful.

I saw that I had come into the world at the moment of history when humans are designed to do certain epochal things — if I do what humans are supposed to be doing, I'm very liable to have some very extraordinary insights that I would not have if I were not operating in absolute faith. If I find my work miraculously supported and if I have important insights that other people don't have, I asked myself, "Can you trust yourself, Bucky, if you have special insights and great technical vision and forecasting capability as a human-affairs navigator and engineer not as a captain, that if you undertake to do certain things and you understand the trend to do more with less; and if you understand what the chemistries are doing, you'll be able to make a great deal of reliable prophecy? Can you count on yourself never, ever to turn this capability to personal advantage — to making money, to revert to saying that you are a special son of God, that you are a guru with some power that other people don't have? Can you trust yourself never to do that?"

I said I am absolutely confident that I can be trusted by God. For this reason, when I am publicly speaking, I always end up remembering that I was a throwaway failure in the accepted rules of earning a living, while playing the "Malthusian inherent-inadequacy-of-life-support-for-all" game.

DIL             In what sense do you use the word "throwaway?"

FULLER          That I found that I could commit suicide; that I had adequate courage to swim out into the lake until I became exhausted and sank. I felt that it would be a great relief from mental anguish. So I said instead of committing suicide, I would take this throwaway and turn all of its experience only into advantage for other people. So I said, "Can you always remember that?" Everytime before I go to sleep, I realize that the individual subconscious and universal evolution is going right on. I close my eyes and say, "Yours, dear God, is *all* the glory."

*Fuller's relationship to God*

I use the word "glory" to mean the total knowledge, wisdom, love and power entering into the fulfillment events of universal evolution. "Yours, dear God, is *all* the glory; though I am being applauded, none of the knowledge and power of the realizations are mine. I have absolute faith and trust in you. I have complete awe of your vision, wisdom and power. I have absolute thankfulness and great joy in it. I love it. I love you, dear God."

Every night before going to sleep, I consider what I really am — *an average human being* regarding which extraordinary phenomenon we don't as yet know much about. The most important thing is that I am an average human being. I am getting many, many letters, from people who are rejoicing in hearing me say that I am not some kind of special human which history has classified as a genius. It is important to everyone to realize that they are born geniuses. Though you cite me with Leonardo . . .

DIL       But they were also average people, in a way . . .

FULLER    They were, they really were. But society tends to make them "genius freaks" as the young people now phrase it. The word genius is ignorant. There is no question about genetics, that is that all humans have vastly more than any of us know.

DIL       I entirely agree with you.

FULLER    So I think one of the reasons for my greatest strength today still is that I have not forgotten who I am.

DIL

The point is that this average person has so much capacity, so much potential, that in the right environment with intelligent effort it is possible to have a wonderful future for all of humankind. This is the hope you give us. Would you say that your hopefulness also has something to do with your happy married life?

FULLER

*Marriage as part of total experience*

Anne and I have been married sixty-six years. So the experience is very great. But I do not make it a special part of my overall experiences. Everything is my total life. Being a mechanic and all those things is equally a part. The phenomenon of love is very mysterious.

DIL

There is no question that you are and always have been loved by your family and friends. What role does love play in the nurturing of the average person who fulfills himself or herself?

FULLER

*The cosmic support of love*

Through all problems of my life, my awareness of the love that I have felt, that I am being loved, that I love others, that I have been loved by others, this, to me, has been the supreme factor that has carried me through many critical moments when I might have otherwise phased out. Love is it. The cosmic support of love, the great mystery of love.

There came a point, in my developing knowledge of and experience with principles that operate physically, at which I came to realize that the eternal principles themselves have such integrity of objectivity in wide ranges of frequency and intensity that they become physical reality itself.

I had an experience with a philosopher, a man who was called a philosopher and professed to be a philosopher. He was a professor of philosophy at a great university.

*Encounter with Professor X*

Many people said to me, "If you ever meet Professor X, he is going to shatter a lot of your working assumptions."

I received an appointment to that university. It was a special short-term fellowship. When I arrived there, the students asked me if I would meet with Professor X on a television program of the university station. I said I would be glad to. So the first and only time I ever met him was at the university television station. The station director sat Professor X and myself on opposite sides of a large wooden table. The director of the program told the professor to start. It was being taped: it was not the live show. The professor started by dramatically and resoundingly pounding the table with his fist saying, "Don't tell me this table isn't solid!" And I said, "How can you see me?" He said, "What do you mean *see* you? You're sitting right there." I said, "You are seeing me through solid glasses. Did you hear me? How can you see through solid glasses? What do you mean by solid?" I went on to recall that all the closely-packed atoms and their electrons are all in motion.

DIL

*Dil's calligraph "Al-Hajar"*

I am so glad to hear this. Yesterday when you were commenting on my calligraph "Al-Hajar," the Arabic word for stone, you especially checked with me to be sure that the calligraph was of the word s-t-o-n-e, and then you said that it was beautiful that it was not a solid. I am sure you must have noticed the movement in the heart of the stone as the central form in my calligraph. It was such a marvelous insight you showed in my conception of the movement in the stone that I wanted to capture in my calligraph.

FULLER

*There are no solids*

The point is that there is a frequency of motion of the atoms and electrons like airplane-propeller blades revolving. You cannot see them, but you cannot put your fist through them, it would get cut off. You can take a machine gun and time it to fire between the revolving blades. In the same way, light can pass between the elec-

98

tron motions of the atoms. If the glass is thick enough, the passing light can get refracted by the atoms to change in angular course. That is how we obtain the correction in our spectacles. I find that everything that we experience is operating on a principle like that and while you and I call it solid, it is not solid at all. Professor X asked the station director to cancel the program and walked out.

What do you say about the idea of love playing an important role in the transformation of the average person's life? That is, that a person who is not in love or who has not had that experience is less likely to be a person who is able to do something with intuition, with aesthetics, and will fail to find hopefulness in his or her life. But a person who is grounded in love of human beings, of nature and the universe in any form, or of God or a divine being, is a person more sensitive toward a certain hopefulness and brightness in life.

FULLER

Well, we all experience many principles operating everywhere around us. For instance, around our planet we have oxygen; we go out from the planet and the oxygen is not there but other phenomena are there, the light from the sun, the light from many stars, billions and quadrillions and quintillions. A little way out we get to the phenomenon we call weightlessness. I spoke last night about Newton's citing what gravity is, the amount of it varying inversely in terms of the second power of the arithmetical distances intervening. That interattraction could be between any two celestial bodies. There are celestial bodies all around us, and they are all integrated with one another according to Newton's Law. As we move further out from Earth's surface, the amount of pull on us by the earth lessens and we gradually become weightless, where the omnidirectional pull on us from the celestial bodies all around us is about equal. As we go out from Earth, which is predominant, the pull is swiftly reduced. Each time we double our distance outwardly from the earth, the pull on us is halved. Professor Goddard noted that the earth is traveling at 66,000 miles an hour around the sun and that each of us is going 66,000 miles per hour. Goddard noted that a body going a little faster would tend to part company with the earth. Goddard does not give you an example, but I point out to you a bicycle lying on the

*Weightlessness*

ground. You stand it vertically and it will keep falling down. But straddle it and pedal it and the faster you get it going, the more vertically stable it becomes. If you pedal fast enough, it tends to leave the earth. Many times my bicycle has jumped across a space. You cannot tip it over at speed because it is trying to leave the earth. Goddard then said that it is shown by Newton's Law, every time we double the distance away from the earth, we halve the amount of the gravitational pull on us to pull us back into the earth. That distance out from the earth, spoken of as "weightlessness" and which I call "critical proximity," is only about a hundred miles out. Now a hundred miles out, in relation to an 8,000-mile-diameter earth, is an almost negligible distance. On my sixty-five-foot long 1/2,000,000 distortion-free one-world-island-in-one-world ocean map which I used in last night's university lecture, one inch is thirty-two miles, so three inches above the map was 100 miles, and that is the height at which powerfully-rocketed bodies go into orbit. That's how close. Only three inches out on my 1/2,000,000 map. At 100 miles

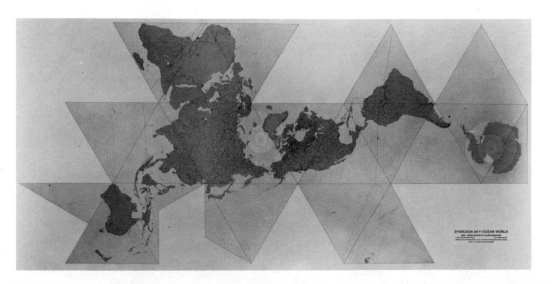

*Buckminster Fuller's One-world-island-in-one-world-ocean map*

out from Earth's surface, the pull of other celestial bodies would be equal to that of the earth, and we mistakenly call it weightlessness.

The universe is cohered by gravity. Each individual physical system of Universe — planet or atom — has its attractive force pulling on its surrounding neighbors as well as its own integral embracing coherence force. The integrity of the universe is this intercohering force which holds it all together. I'm going to give you a graphic way of comprehending gravity and radiation. All structural systems in Universe are always coping with radiant forces of expansion and with embracing forces of contraction.

The individual system's individual, system-interrelating, structural components are continually subjected to forces against which they push or pull to withstand the integrative contraction forces of gravity and the disintegrative

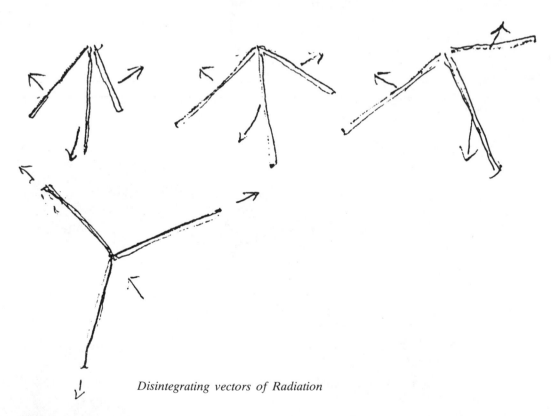

Disintegrating vectors of Radiation

explosive forces of radiation. In engineering, we find that we can deal very discretely with these push-pull forces by treating these forces as its vectors. Vectors are lines the length of which are the product of the mass multiplied by the velocity of the force involved, which vector is aimed in a specific angular direction in respect to a given axis of reference.

We will now take six, six-feet-long-each, three-fourths-inch-diameter aluminum tubes, each tube representing one vector. Three of them we employ as a tripod, hinge-fastening together their three top ends in the manner of a camera tripod's top-jointing. The tripod's legs' three feet try to slide apart from one another on a polished marble floor. To prevent their traveling apart we take the other three six-foot aluminum tubes and string them together with a dacron cord running through the tubes and tied together at one of the joints to form an aluminum tube triangle. These vectors are tensionally cohered with one another at both ends of each other to form a closed polygon. The three aluminum tube vectors in the tripod being fastened to one another at only one end each are disintegrative as their centers of gravity tend to recede from one another. As such they act as radiants.

Gravity and radiation

What we have learned here is that Universe has divided all its energy into two equal parts and has invested one part in divergent radial expansion and the other half in contractive convergence − gravity.

But the convergent gravity's energy-patterning arrangement of fastening together both ends of each vector to produce a closed, inherently integrative polygon is twice as effective as is the radiant-disintegrative patterning, thus insuring the eternal superiority of gravity over radiation.

The integrity of the universe is that gravity holds all together. And I'm going to give you an example of gravity − and everything is push and pull, and the tendency to

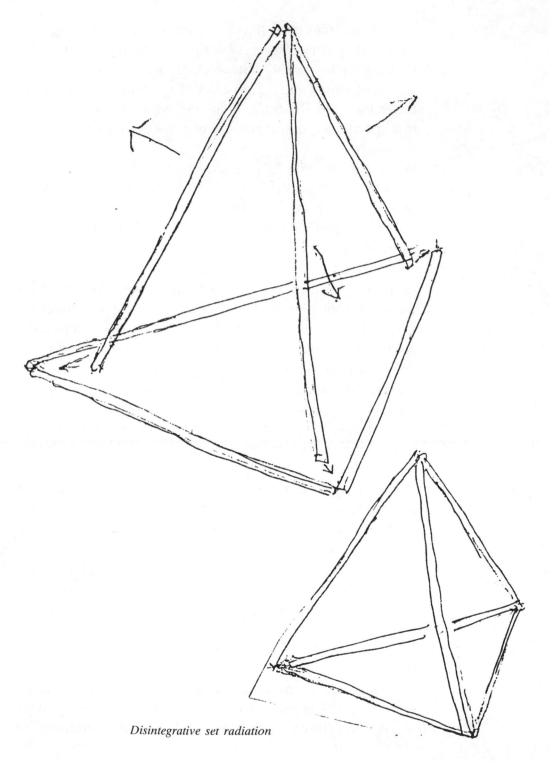

*Disintegrative set radiation*

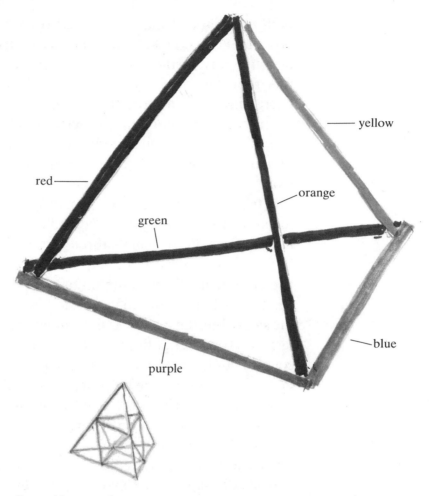

*Green, blue, purple energy photosynthetically integrative as biologic hydro matter*

*Energy associative gravitationally as crystalline matter*

push and pull. All structure has push and pull. I'm going to take a camera tripod with three legs and they are fastened together only at the top. So the bottom ends of those legs try to spread apart. These three trying-to-spread-apart legs represent the disintegrative radiation. But we also take three other legs of exactly the same size as the camera tripod legs and fasten them together at both ends, and it makes a closed triangle. With the tripod's feet placed inside the triangle the tripod's legs cannot slide any further apart. These three integrative vectors represent the gravity of the universe. So that the energy invested in these three legs, which we call vectors in structural mathematics, exactly equals the amount of energy invested in the tripod's three vector-disintegrating radiation. Radiation is disintegrative; gravity is integrative.

The tripod representing the radiation of Universe is fastened together at only one end and its other ends are disintegrative. The triangle's three vectors are integratively fastened together at both ends. The gravity is integrative and embracing. So the amount of energy invested in Universe in radiation and that invested in gravity are exactly the same, but the gravity is used more efficiently by being fastened together at both ends forming a closed system in contradiction to radiation's disintegrating systems.

Gravity guarantees the integrity of eternally-regenerative Universe, so we find that with radiation we can put a reflector behind it, we can beam and focus radiation.

*Gravity as physical love*

Radiation has shadows; on the other hand, I find this omni-embracing gravity cannot be focused and has no pure shadows. I spoke to you of experiences happening in pure principle, embracing and permeative metaphysical love. Gravity is omni-embracing and permeative; gravity is physical love. The metaphysical embracement of our universe is love; cosmic integrity is love. That is why only love can take us through the supreme troubles.

| | |
|---|---|
| DIL | How do you define love in these terms? |
| FULLER<br><br>*Fuller's definition<br>of personal love* | I define the personal experience of love as the special case, generalized integrity of Universe. As I have now said a number of times, I call God the intellectual integrity of the universe. To really understand such concepts, we have to have at least four repeatings. |
| DIL | From this perspective, then, love of God, Universe, humankind is an integral element in the fulfillment of human personality. Love of nature, love of one's self . . . |
| FULLER | I don't call it love of oneself. I call that crass. I hear a lot of people say that. |
| DIL<br><br>*Love of Self* | What would you say about one's own personal identity and one's awareness and cultivation of one's own individual, unique self? I use the term "love of one's self" in the sense of one's self-understanding, self-affirmation, self-development, and self-expression in order for a person to become a worthwhile and fulfilling being. Of course, a natural and simultaneous component of such awareness of one's unique selfhood is the merging of this uniquely-individual cultivated self into the larger social and cosmic self so that each dimension strengthens and enriches the other. There are poets and philosophers like . . . |
| FULLER<br><br>*Love-of-self poets* | I first wish to respond to "love-of-self" poets. Because a poet has said something in poetry does not make it true. I pointed out to you yesterday that life begins with awareness of otherness. I have pointed out that radiation is disintegrative and that gravity is integrative. Love can become integrative only with the otherness. What I think you and your poets are talking about is self-appreciation. I think what is masked as "self-love" hides selfishness, greed, pride and fear. |

As poetry about love, I think that this one from the New
Testament profoundly supports what I conceive love to
be:

The Lord our God is one Lord.
The first law is
Thou shalt love
The Lord thy God
With all thy heart
With all thy soul
With all thy mind
And with all thy strength
This is the First Commandment
And the Second is like
Namely this
Thou shalt love
Thy neighbor as thyself
There is none other commandment
Greater than these
Upon these two
Stand all the law and the prophets.

The King James Version of the Bible
St. Mark 12: 29−31;

The first of all the commandments *is*,
The Lord our God is one Lord:
And thou shalt love the Lord thy God
with all thy heart, and with all thy strength:
this *is* the first commandment.
And the second *is* like, *namely* this,
Thou shalt love thy neighbor as thyself.
There is none other commandment greater than these.

In my book *Intuition* I wrote what was acclaimed as poetry by an Iranian scholar of ancient Persian poetry.

Love
Is omni-inclusive,
Progressively exquisite,
Understanding and tender
And compassionately attuned
To other than self.

*Macrocosmically* speaking
Experience teaches
Both the fading away
Of remote yesterdays
And the unseeability
Of far forward events.
*Microcosmically* speaking
Science has proven
The absolutely exact
Also to be
Humanly unreachable,
For all acts of measuring
Alter that which is measured.

Conceptual totality
Is inherently prohibited.
But exactitude can be bettered
And measurement refined
By progressively reducing
Residual errors,
Thereby disclosing
The directions of truths
Ever progressing
Toward the eternally exact
Utter perfection,
Complete understanding,
Absolute wisdom,

Unattainable by humans
But affirming God
Omnipermeative,
Omniregenerative,
All incorruptible
As infinitely inclusive
Exquisite love.

While humans may never
Know God directly
They may have and do
Palpitatingly hover
Now towards, now away.
And some in totality
Come closer to God.

And whole ages of peoples
In various places
Leave average records
Of relative proximities
Attained toward perfection.

PERSIA — positioned
At demographical center
Of all Earthian peoples —
Has been traversed by many
Into and beyond
The vanishing past
And will be traversed by many
Into and beyond
The foreseeable future.

And at this most crisscrossed
Crossroads of history
The record is left
Of the relative proximity
Averagingly attained
To that which is God.

The PERSIANS' record
Is tender and poignant
Sheltering, embracing,
An omnipoetical
Proximity to God.

Garden,
Shah Abbas Inn
Isfahan
September 6, 1970

Four years before writing my poem on love in Isfahan, I was appointed to design the United States Pavilion for the 1967 Montreal World Fair. My Expo '67 dome and the other four buildings were built on an island in St. Lawrence River just east of the city of Montreal. They had built a tunnel from the city to the island. The tunnel exit on the island was just in front of the United States Pavilion. On the opening day of the fair, I stood with my wife Anne at that tunnel exit. As the people emerged, the first thing they could see was my dome. Almost all of them ejaculated: "How beautiful!"

To Anne this seemed to give sublime validation to the extraordinary backing she had given me throughout the fifty years since our World War I marriage.

When I was a little boy my mother used to tell me about the Taj Mahal and showed me pictures of it. She felt it to be the most beautiful building in all the world and she felt its beauty went beyond its structural exquisiteness. She felt that the real beauty was mystical — it sprang from the love of its builder for his wife.

Both Anne and Allegra know that in 1927 I gave up entirely the idea of trying to use my capabilities to develop special economic and physical advantage for them, and instead committed myself to the proposition that if those whom I love were indeed the kind of human beings I thought them to be, they would not like finding themselves in a position of special economic and physical advantage won at the cost of deprivation of others, and, likewise, their true happiness could only develop through an awareness that our efforts were always in the direction of progressively-increasing advantage for all humans, without any biases whatsoever.

Because every action has its reaction and resultant, and because no event in Universe can be independent of the rest of Universe, my commitment in the direction of all humanity and its present symbolic embodiment in my

*The Taj Mahal*

*"Anne's Taj Mahal." Fuller's name for the geodesic dome he designed for the United States Pavilion at Expo '67 in Montreal.*

*The geodesic dome house that Bucky and Anne Fuller built in Carbondale, Illinois, 1960.*

*Fuller in the library on the second floor in the dome house.*

114

*Bucky and Anne Fuller in their geodesic house, 1960.*

Expo '67 dome, though dedicated to all humanity, must have its inadvertently complementary involvement of Anne and Allegra as well.

I said to Anne at Montreal, "In addition to the geodesic dome which I have designed here to demonstrate doing so much more with less for all humanity that world man will realize intuitively that his salvation and physical success on the spaceship Earth is to be gained by such a design revolution and not by political revolution, I have inadvertently brought about the production and installation of our own Taj as pure fallout of my love for you." She knew it was so. Our Expo Taj is powerful and the beauty goes far beyond the sum of its physical parts.

*Anne Fuller's accident*

Anne and I left the dome and flew from Montreal to New York City. I was to leave her with her family at their old home on Long Island. On the way from Kennedy Airport to New York City the taxi we were riding in skidded at high speed in the rain and we crashed against a bridge abutment and bounced across the highway. Neither the taxicab driver nor I were hurt but Anne was very greatly damaged. She had two hemorrhages in the brain. Three weeks later, after a successful operation, she was at last recovering consciousness and apparently had complete mental clarity.

*Gene Fowler's letter to Fuller on love and Anne's "Taj Mahal"*

One June 6, 1967 when I wrote about all the foregoing to my poet friend Gene Fowler of San Francisco, she had just been taken from the intensive-care ward to a private room at the University Hospital in New York City. On June 13, Gene wrote back to me as follows:

Dear Bucky:

Anne is a woman of considerable strength: she will not leave you to continue alone.

I have known a long time that Anne's strength, beauty and grace were in your work — it makes sense that this skybreak bubble should be, not a monument, but an em-

116

bodiment of your love of her. Isn't that love a carrier wave that brought her form and substance, her nature and patterning into and through you and into your visions and work? Isn't a human being a thin, sparkling transparent membrane reaching out and containing, for a time some part of the universe.

Human beings are fragile skybreak bubbles, as vulnerable and quickly gone as a child's soap bubbles in a bath. Yet, without vulnerability, there is no courage. Without mortality, there is no beauty or love, no reason to reach out and touch.

You've constructed something slightly tougher than a human being, but with the same beauty and grace, a knowing set into materials torn from our Earth and shaped through our fires and minds, a memory to outlast the one remembered and the one remembering, a knowing of a woman, of Woman, a knowing large enough to be seen from space, a knowing men may enter and share.

More than the Taj, Bucky,
With love,
Gene

DIL

Beautiful! I agree with Gene Fowler that Anne is a woman of extraordinary strength and her beauty and grace are in your work. This is the sixty-sixth year of your wedding anniversary and I wish you both many more years of healthy and inspired life together.

*Dil's poem to his wife*

Two years back I wrote a short poem for Afia on our twentieth wedding anniversary.

*Sunflower*

A part of
    the earth's rotation
    round the distant star,

The sunflower
>    has an added movement all its own.

This relation
>    that no other flower —
>    not even the rose —
>    can claim,

Makes bold the sunflower
>    to ask the sun:
>    "What is it that is between
>    you and me alone, my friend?"

San Diego, California
March 14, 1981

What might interest you is that when I read this poem to Afia she thought she was the sunflower, because in the classical Indian poetic tradition it is the woman who is the lover and the man the beloved.

*Iqbal's poetry and philosophy*

But let me return to our discussion of self and self-transcendence or what I prefer to call the "I — and — We Equation." What I was going to talk about was of two Persian poems by Muhammad Iqbal, the poet-philosopher of Pakistan. His *Asrar-e Khudi* (The Secrets of Self) published in 1915, and *Rumuz-e Bekhudi* (The Mysteries of Self-Transcendence) published in 1918, precisely addressed the question of resolving the classic problem you identified in your usage of the term "self-love" which very often serves as a mask for selfishness, greed and pride. Iqbal was interested in awakening his people through a message of self-understanding and self-development for becoming worthy individuals as a necessary condition toward establishing an ideal society, the kingdom of God on earth. An individual for him was a finite center of human experience, who aspires to a unity with other finite centers, and thereby transcends to its ultimate unity in the Infinite, God.

118

*Muhammad Iqbal*
*Sketch by Aslam Kamal, Lahore, Pakistan.*

To quote Iqbal from his introductory note in *Asrar*: "To my mind, this inexplicable finite centre of experience is the fundamental fact of the universe. All life is individual; there is no such thing as universal life. God Himself is an individual: He is the most unique individual."[28]
Iqbal sees humans in Universe evolving from "chaos to cosmos." In this movement toward ultimate uniqueness, which is God, the human personality is strengthened by love:

The luminous point whose name is the Self
Is the life-spark beneath our dust.

By love it is made more lasting,
More living, more burning, more glowing.
From love proceeds the radiance of its being
And the development of its unknown possibilities.
Its nature gathers fire from Love,
Love instructs it to illumine the world.[29]

It is this love-inspired self of the individual human that becomes the vital link between what has gone before and what is to come in the universe. And through such merging of the individual self in the community, humans can fulfill their function in the universe. Life is thus defined by Iqbal in *Rumuz* as a wave of consciousness of continuity.[30]

A community comprising such individuals bonded together in love becomes "like the light of God," which functions at three levels, as Iqbal states in his *Javid Nama* (1930): first, man's self-awareness so he sees himself in his own light; second, the consciousness of another so he can see himself in another's light; and third, his consciousness of God's essence, so he can see himself in the light of God's essence.[31] Iqbal's conception of religion is thus "to awaken in man the higher consciousness of his manifold relations with God and the universe" and thus man is conceived as a creative activity, an ascending spirit who, in his onward march, rises from one state of being to another, from the individual to the social to the divine.[32]

*Other philosophers on love in Universe* This is what in essence Pierre Teilhard de Chardin also says in his book *The Phenomenon of Man,*[33] that love is the affinity of life in all forms. Unless there is a real internal propensity to this cosmic unity and oneness, it is not possible for love to appear in the "hominized" form. Love is thus a fundamental universal principle. This is what de Chardin calls gravity at work in the universe. His concept of "within" of beings is what in essence Iqbal meant by his term "Khudi" or "Self."

As I see it, Martin Buber's concept of "Ich und Du" (I and Thou)[34] is rooted in the convergence of what he calls "meetings" or "relations" in Universe.

While Muhammad Iqbal, Teilhard de Chardin and Martin Buber represent the best of the Islamic, Christian and Judaic traditions of knowledge and wisdom in our time, I find the same current of thought in the work of Radhakrishnan of Hinduism, Suzuki of Buddhism, and some other contemporary thinkers — a coming-together of all humans in Universe through the principle of love of humankind and God.

*Einstein on religion and enlightenment*

This is what we were talking about earlier in the context of Einstein's faith: "A person who is religiously enlightened appears to me to be one who has, to the best of his ability, liberated himself from the fetters of his selfish desires and is preoccupied with thoughts, feelings, and aspirations to which he clings because of their super-personal value. It seems to me that what is important is the force of this personal content and the depth of the conviction concerning its overpowering meaningfulness, regardless of whether any attempt is made to unite this content with a divine being, for otherwise it would not be possible to count Buddha and Spinoza as religious personalitics."[35] It is this kind of mind, according to Einstein, that is capable of larger and deeper understanding of life and the universe.

*"The basic word I-You can be spoken only with one's whole being. The concentration and fusion into a whole being can never be accomplished by me, can never be accomplished without me. I require a You to become; becoming I, I say You.*
*All actual life is encounter.*

*. . .*

*Spirit in its human manifestation is man's response to his You. Man speaks in many tongues — tongues of language, of art, of action — but the spirit is one; it is response to the You that appears from the mystery and addresses us from the mystery. Spirit is word. And even as verbal speech may first become word in the brain of man and then become sound in his throat, although both are merely refractions of the true event because in truth language does not reside in man but man stands in language and speaks out of it — so it is with all words, all spirit. Spirit is not in the I but between I and You. It is not like the blood that circulates in you but like the air in which you breathe. Man lives in the spirit when he is able to respond to his You. He is able to do that when he enters into this relation with his whole being. It is solely by virtue of his power to relate that man is able to live in the spirit."*
*— Martin Buber's I and Thou.*
*Translated by Walter Kaufmann.*
*New York: Charles Scribner's Sons, 1970, pp. 62, 89.*


*"Everywhere on earth, at this moment, within the new spiritual atmosphere created by the appearance of the idea of evolution, there float — in a state of extreme mutual sensitivity — the two essential components of the Ultra-human, love of God and faith in the world. Everywhere these two components are 'in the air': generally, however, they are not strong enough, both at the same time, to combine with one another in one and the same subject. In me, by pure chance (temperament, education, environment) the*

*proportion of each happens to be favourable, and they fuse together spontaneously. The fusion of the two is still not strong enough to spread explosively, but even so it is enough to show that such an explosion is possible and that,* sooner or later the chain-reaction will get under way.

*It is one more proof that if the truth appears once, in one single mind, that is enough to ensure that nothing can ever prevent it from spreading to everything and setting it ablaze."*

— *Pierre Teilhard de Chardin's* Le Christique, *March 1955.* Teilhard de Chardin Album, *edited by Jeanne Mortier and Marie-Louise Aboux. New York: Harper & Row, 1966, p. 210.*

*"All religions require us to look upon life as an opportunity for self-realization — atmanastu kamaya. They call upon us to strive incessantly and wrest the immortal from the mortal. God is the universal reality, wisdom and love and we are His children irrespective of race or religious belief. Within each incarnate soul dwells the god-consciousness which we must seek out and awaken. When mankind awakes to the truth, universal brotherhood will follow, the at-one-ment with the great fountainhead of all creation. One whose life is rooted in the experience of the Supreme spontaneously develops love for all creation.*
. . .
*A religion which brings together the divine revelation in nature and history with the inner revelation in the life of the spirit can serve as the basis of the world order, as the religion of the future. Whatever point of view we start from, Hindu or Muslim, Buddhist or Christian, if we are sincere in our intention and earnest in our effort, we get to the Supreme. We are members of the one Invisible Church of God or one Fellowship of the Spirit, though we may belong to this or that visible Church."*

— *S. Radhakrishnan's* Religion and Culture. *Delhi: Hind Pocket Books, 1968, pp. 15, 18—19.*

*"The climax of Buddhist philosophy is reached in the Keg-on conception of Jiji-mu-ge (literally, each thing no hindrance). As I see it, this is the summit of oriental thought as developed by the finest Buddhist minds, and represents Japan's contribution to world philosophy. Kegon philosophy teaches a four-fold conception of the world: (1) The world viewed as individual existences; (2) The world viewed as the Absolute; (3) The world conceived as individuals retaining their individuality in the Absolute, and (4) The world conceived as each revealed through each other, so that each individual has no hindrance from being merged in every other . . .*

*When the world is so conceived it ceases to be a mere world of the senses, and becomes the spiritual world which Buddhists call the Dharma-loka. If the notion of a physical world is retained, each individual will lose its ultimate significance, but in a spiritual world all which was lost is restored. Each individual is asserted to exist, and the physical world is restored, but this time as a spiritual world. In Christian terminology, it reflects, the divine glory. The earth acquires heavenly splendour and this world of misery becomes a land of purity, or the Pure Land."*
— *Daisetz Teitaro Suzuki's* The Essence of Buddhism. *English translation of the Command Address to H. M. The Emperor of Japan on April 23—24, 1946. London: The Buddhist Society, 1971, pp. 93—94.*

FULLER

I respect deeply your response to my statement about love. I classify the thoughts of other thinkers which you have submitted as appreciations of the significance of self.

*Unity being plural and at minimum two*

I would like to support my viewpoint with a poem that I wrote two months ago. Before you read it, I would like to point out that in 1944 I was told by the head of the British Scientific Office in Washington, D. C. participating in

124

the Manhattan Project that my dissertation on unity being plural and at minimum two inspired the Manhattan Project scientists to apply it to quantum mechanics, which rendered the latter powerfully effective in their nuclear calculations.


*At Minimum Two*

Synergy is
the complex behavior
of whole systems
unpredictable by
the isolated observation
and consideration
of only one or more
parts of the system.

Love is the synergy
of omnipermeative
and inherently differentiating
metaphysical radiation
nonsynchronously coexisting
with omniembracing
and systemically integrating,
eternally conserving,
metaphysical gravity.

Metaphysical radiation
and metaphysical gravity
eternally and only
coexist.

The always and only coexistent
positive and negative mathematics
demonstrated scientifically
that unity is plural
and at minimum two.

In its inherent cell dichotomy,
biology demonstrates
that unity is plural
and at minimum two.

Science demonstrates
that unity is plural and at minimum two
with its life-initiating
awareness of otherness.
No otherness, no awareness.
No life.
Life is inherently two.

Science again demonstrates
that unity is plural
and at minimum two
by requiring
both an insideness and outsideness
of both
the observed and the observer.

Science again demonstrates that unity
is at minimum two
in the concomitant,
always and only coexisting
convexity and concavity.
Science demonstrates
that convexity diffuses
and concavity concentrates
the same impinging radiation
wherefore the always and only
coexisting concavity and convexity
demonstrate that they are not
the same function
wherefore unity is plural
and at minimum two.

The eternally convergent-divergent
dissynchronous juxtapositioning
of inherently dissipative radiation
and inherently conserving gravity
pulsatively and resonatively propagate
the infinite variety
of wavelengths and frequencies
of nonsimultaneous, differently enduring,
only overlappingly episoded,
only locally aborning and dying
and only sumtotally
eternally regenerative
scenario Universe.

Appreciation of the integrity
of eternally regenerative, scenario Universe
is sometimes called "Wisdom."

Employment of
the only metaphysically experienced,
eternally regenerative scenario Universe
is sometimes identified as "Love."

Unity of Universe is always plural
and in its minimum twofoldedness
as both Wisdom and Love,
these two synergize
to constitute the phenomenon
we intuitively identify
as God.

This is probably as close
as we may ever come
to such human-thought identifying.

Penang, Malaysia
February 14, 1983
St. Valentine's Day/ Chinese New Year

FULLER

*Life is
metaphysical*

At eighty-seven years of age, I have consumed 300 tons of food, air and water which became my flesh, hair et al. to be entirely rubbed out and cut off — to join other systems. I am convinced that neither you nor I are the food we eat. I took off seventy pounds and said, "Who was that?" I am convinced that neither humans nor God are physical. Our bodies consist entirely of atoms. Atoms are entirely inanimate. Whatever life may be, it is weightless, metaphysical.

*"I took off seventy pounds and said, 'Who was that?'"
Photo by John A. Blume.*

DIL

Dr. Fuller, we seem to have reached a stage in our exploration where I would like to ask you the question: What is the essential content of the emotional, intellectual, and spiritual "baggage" that human beings are to carry into the twenty-first century, as we approach it? We seem to be carrying so much dead weight.

FULLER

*The importance of mind*

I have already pointed out to you that human beings have a faculty that no other creature has, which is mind. Other creatures have brains, as do humans. And I have found we have minds with access to some of the great generalized principles of the universe. We have arrived at the awareness of that which is a long way from our having always been deliberately born naked, helpless, without any experience, therefore, utterly ignorant. We are given drives of thirst and hunger, curiosity, to learn only by trial and error. We have come to an extraordinary moment in history where we have acquired an awareness of being able to differentiate between brain and mind. I am able to do this only because at this moment in history, things I have been able to do I could not have done earlier. There was that point in history when, having parted with tradition, I set about to discover what Universe is trying to do and that differs from what humanity's most powerful political and economic leaders are trying to do. I start by trying to determine what I have as equipment and therewith to discover what Universe is and why it included humans, and further, to discover where human beings are in this moment in history and evolution. If I hadn't done this, someone else would have done it. The moment had come when somebody had to do it.

Evolution, then, is in incredible acceleration because of the discovery of exponential inter-implementing of technology. Our evolutionary acceleration is demonstrably four-dimensional. The fourth power. Things are happening just in this minute we sit here that would have taken thousands of years to transpire a few centuries ago. This conversation we are having could not have taken place ever before. I find that to me, humans are at a point in history where we now have the capability to forever dispense with learning only by trial and error how to survive. The earning-a-living requirement is about to be eliminated. I see human individuals able to make so many mistakes now having made the greatest mistake, wherein all the great religious and political systems have concluded and decreed that "nobody should make mistakes." And that we must punish all those who make mistakes. It is only by mistakes that we can learn. We have been doing many right things but always for the wrong reasons. We have come into enough knowledge so that now we are going to be required by Universe to do the right things for the right reasons.

*On making mistakes*

Our present anti-mistake-making laws and customs tend to frustrate our further growth. Humanity is taught to play the game by the rules and not by thinking. So if anti-thinking is dominant, we may be all through. I am assuming that we were introduced into Universe to do the local thinking essential to our support of the integrity of eternally-regenerative Universe.

*Nature's fail-safe circuitry*

I guess there must be some other experiments, in thinking-capable individuals, going on elsewhere. Nature always has alternate fail-safe circuitry. She cannot be dependent on this one little colonization on this one little planet Earth.

I think this particular Earthian colonization is in a final examination to see whether we humans have the intellectual integrity of initiative to go with our minds or are we going to go with our crowd psychology brains. To me the most promising phenomenon is that we have been able to see some real gains of humanity, clearly established, real breakthroughs.

The fathers and mothers of children born throughout history have been the immediate authority regarding what the children can safely eat and what they can do without getting into trouble with the system around them. The father and mother were the immediate authority. And the mother was tied by her womb-carrying to a small geographical circle. The father could travel, so he became the hunter, one way or another, he covered more geography than the mother. Therefore, he had more news to bring home. Mom talked about social principles to the kids, and Dad talked about the physical news — what the king in the next kingdom said he's going to do, and so forth. Dad told it to the children in his own esoteric, very-bad-language way. The children understood him, but his and his children's mouthings gave rise to many, many dialects.

Suddenly, in the evolution of learning principles and that invisible technological revolution I spoke about, in 1927 all the daddies of the world were coming home and the kids said, "Daddy, come listen to the radio, a man is flying across the Atlantic!" And Daddy never brought home the news ever again. He lost that incredibly important function and its authority. The people who got their jobs on the radio did so by virtue of the commonality of their diction rather than the esoteric way in which Daddy said it. The radio voices had also better and larger vocabularies and the capability to use those words spontaneously. The children saw Dad and Mom who were their authority go to the neighbors and say, "Listen to the radio, what the man is telling." So, quite clearly, the children's authority, the parents, were declaring that the people on the radio were an even greater authority. Since the people on the radio were saying it this way, the kids said the greater authority says it this way, so we'll emulate it.

The average workman, sixty years before we had any radio, had a vocabulary of only a few hundred words. The average six-year-old child today has a vocabulary in the neighborhood of five thousand words.

This is an incredible breakthrough in the integrity of the resources of the mind.

*The dissident generation*

In the mid-sixties we had many dissident college and university student eruptions. These dissident students often invited me to come and meet with them, particularly the ones at University of California at Berkeley. We found that they were born the year the television came into the American home.

The speed of sound is approximately 700 miles per hour. The speed of light is nearly 700 million miles per hour. The sound stops at the limit of the atmosphere. Electromagnetic communication (light) travels on eternally. The information that we can get with our eyes via television can be one million times greater in range and speed than via our ears and the radio. So here is a new generation, getting world-around and local universe information with both their eyes and ears. They said to me, "My mother and father love me very much, and I love them very much, but they don't know what's going on." The world is in great trouble as the television is telling us about the whole world. These 1965 dissident university students said to me, "My father and mother don't have anything to do with anything. They come home and have a beer and go to the television, but they don't know what to do about the world's troubles. They have no idea what is really going on in the world. They don't know anything about going to Korea, they don't know anything about going to the moon. So we've got to do our own thinking because the world is in trouble."

Consider, Dr. Dil, how this contrasts to the time when I was a child and my mother would say, "Never mind what you think, listen, we're trying to teach you."

Suddenly the young people are discovering that the older people can't teach them, or are teaching them misinformation. They had to find out for themselves. So suddenly it became incumbent upon a whole generation of youth to do its own thinking. Universe said to them, "Hair is coming out here, I don't know why we have hair at all. But since it is trying to come out I had better let it do so." They let the hair come out. The older people did not understand at all, they thought they were being perverse. It was incredible integrity, trying to do their own thinking.

Then they found themselves being exploited due to their idealism. And they found they were using their heads as battering rams in political causes without meaning. They said, "We've got to get over that." So they now have developed complete immunity to political issues. So we're having this breakthrough into a new world that arrived via technology, and the technology came via the understanding of principles which human mind discovered.

*The "post-moon-landers"*

Next we have another incredible breakthrough. We have the moon-landing. The moon had been there for whatever number of years the humans have been here, which we now know to be at least three-and-a-half million years. And the moon symbolized everything humans could never reach.

I'm finding what I call the "post-moon-landers," now thirteen or less years of age, writing me letters. The post-moon-landers are very aware of all the complexities of things that had to be done to get to the moon and back safely. It was the first big project of many billions of government dollars that had ever been undertaken in advanced technology that wasn't obviously undertaken for war.

Behind it there were space-age conflict anticipations, but that was not the dramatic objective, which was just taking us to the moon and back.

Now these thirteen-years-later post-moon-landing-born humans are saying in their letters to me, "Humanity can do anything it wants to do, why don't we make the world work for everybody?"

I will give you one more encouraging aspect of evolution, which is that each child born successively is born in the presence of less misinformation. I was born in the presence of my elders saying it was inherently impossible for man to fly. It was inherently impossible to get to the North Pole, or the South Pole, and all those things. Each child born successively is also born in the presence of a little more reliable information. We have come to a new generation which knows that if you can go to the moon and back safely, you can do anything you need to do technologically provided you do it in a big enough way and pay the bills.

So I find that the young world now doing its own thinking is doing so in a very big way. It is considering that it can do anything. In five years, the post-moon-landers will be eighteen. In three more years, they will be at the age at which Alexander became Alexander the Great as he conquered the world. The post-moon-landers are the realization of the Biblical "And a little child shall lead them." As Alexander conquered with the sword, they are going to conquer the world with their minds. So my hopes are predicated entirely on the competent initiative of the young world. And I think we will probably make the breakthrough due to the sanity and the clarity of the thinking of the young world.[36]

DIL

In order for these young people to be what you hope that they will, what would be your message to the parents and the children of the world?

FULLER

My message to the parents is: Please let the children do their own thinking. Honor their thinking and their initiatives.

DIL                 What would you say in one sentence to the teachers of
                    the world?

FULLER              Well, I don't know who they are. There are a whole lot of
                    people earning their living being professional teachers. I
                    don't counsel other people, sir, I don't do that.
                    People ask me these things you have asked. Everything I
                    have said to you today I have written before. I've never
                    had an instance, however, of a human being with both the
                    capability and the care to ask me the questions you have
                    asked me. I think we have made a valuable recording. In
                    whatever time we have been at it, we have been able to
                    get in all the main ideas it has taken me twenty-two books
                    to express. It has taken me thousands of hours of lectur-
                    ing to try to communicate these thoughts.

DIL                 Would you at this point make a statement that you have
                    not written? What would that be?

FULLER              One of the things that interests me is something strange
                    that occurs on every occasion of my making a scientific
*Woman in*          and socially-advantageous discovery and the special-case
*Fuller's life*     technological invention therefrom, in general support of
                    my attempting to solve human problems with technol-
                    ogy.
                    Whatever the discovery and invention may be, I have al-
                    ways had the experience of some, to me, enchanting fe-
                    male coming into my life concurrently with the scientific
                    discovery.
                    You, Anwar, have brought my darling wife into our dis-
                    cussion. Despite flirtations and sex with others, I have
                    never stopped loving my wife above all others. What I am
                    getting at here is the Iliad- and Odyssey- or Aeneid-like
                    sirens or other females' interception of the explorer's
                    route. This has repeated itself a number of times in my
                    life. Every time I am about to make a discovery and am

developing a high sensitivity of thinking, along comes, to me, an exceptionally charming female with whom I find myself tending to fall in love. Only when I have successfully restrained myself from falling further and have applied myself exclusively to the discovery or inventing, only then do the critically-relevant conceptions occur which secure my comprehension of the significance of the discovering and/or inventing and what my responsibilities are in making the discovery and inventions effectively available to humanity.

*Recirculating human life*

I have come to the conclusion that human life coming out of the woman can recirculate for generations, while gaining critical experience but not taking innovative initiatives or making any cosmic discoveries. I can see sex, per se, as the male attempting to re-enter the womb, endeavoring to rejoin the umbilical cord, to be recirculated for further generations in order to avoid taking evolution-advancing initiatives and thereby taking on socially new and strange responsibilities.

At any rate, that is something I have never written before, for which mental sortie you asked me. I suspect it may be importantly true. I think that nature very clearly wants to let people make mistakes and not get too discouraged by them.

*Woman as the continuum of human life*

You have a copy of my piece on integrity wherein I wrote that only women can conceive, gestate, and bear both male and female humans. Women are the continuum of human life. Like the tension of gravity-cohering space-islanded galaxies, stars, planets and atoms, women are continuous. Men are discontinuous space islands. Men, born forth only from the wombs of women, have the function of activating women's reproductivity.

Nature had to have a capability to continually make new babies, some of them gradually developing genetically to conceive new technologies. After the metaphysical humans have invented mechanical substitutes for all their physical components, then the forever-mysterious metaphysical human (mind) may travel elsewhere on a great new cosmic mission.

The connection between the rights of women and the atomic holocaust may at first seem remote, but I am confident that the holocaust can be prevented only by individual humans demonstrating uncompromising integrity in all matters, thus qualifying us for continuance in the semi-divine designing initiative bestowed upon us in the gift of our mind.

DIL

*Iqbal on Woman*

The subject of love in relation to moments of high sensitivity of thinking and imagination is perennial. I am reminded of a stanza in Iqbal's *Javid Nama* I referred to earlier:

Woman is the guardian of the fire of life,
her nature is the tablet of life's mysteries;
she strikes our fire against her own soul
and it is her substance that makes of the dust a man.

In her heart lurk life's potentialities,
from her glow and flame life derives stability;
she is a fire from which the sparks break forth,
body and soul, lacking her glow, cannot take shape.

What worth we possess derives from her values
for we are all images of her fashioning:
if God has bestowed on you a glance aflame
cleanse yourself, and behold her sanctity.[37]

The joy of creation is like "fire in the body." Rabindranath Tagore says while paying tribute to Valmiki, the author of the Indian epic *Ramayana*, that one who is blessed with the divine joy of creation is full of the awakening of ecstasy. This gift is like fire that burns in his heart day and night, and while it burns his being it gives light to the world.

137

*Fuller lecturing in Radio City Music Hall, New York, 1979.*

*The Dartmouth Conference in Leningrad held under the auspices of the Soviet Academy of Sciences in 1964 to discuss problems existing between the USA and the USSR. At the final session, Fuller (fourth from left) was chosen to speak on behalf of the US delegation.*

I think this is quite a wonderful day. The time had to come in my life wherein the average human being that I am — is doing what I am doing, and is being effective, at which moment a beautiful man such as you would ask me these questions. So this has been a beautiful moment. That you have been able to record it is very important. I would very much like to have a copy of the recording. I would like to say something more. What we have experienced together today — I want to say to you that there had to come a moment in my life when after writing many, many books, and given many, many lectures, that there would be someone capable of asking me the sort of questions you have asked me. And be able to get it all

*Fuller compliments Dil on his questions and suggests the present volume*

*Fuller's published works, July 1, 1983.*
*Photo by Wilbur T. Blume.*

into a really short session and record it. Remembering that I am what I am, and that I represent really an evolutionary event, which might have happened to somebody else, so that I am not kidding myself about where I am at all. I made it very clear that it all is a great mystery. But there had to come a time when I would be able to have somebody interrogate me by experience-evolved knowledge, capable of interrogating me about the important points. So we could condense everything that is important into a very short period. I never had so much communication in so little time. With the communicating so capably evolved, as to bring out exactly what is essential to comprehension of humanity's present evolutionary status, I would like very much, if you agree, to have it transcribed. Transcriptions always turn out to be very disappointing. There is a mysterious difference between written and spoken syntax. Transcriptions tend to make the speakers appear to be idiots, so the transcription will have to be translated and verified. After it is transcribed I'll do my correcting of it and you may do your correcting of your part. It would be very appropriate to have it in a book. I would like us to be co-authors of it.

DIL            Thank you, Dr. Fuller. You do me a great honor.

At this point let me show you some of my paintings including the ones you showed particular interest in last evening. I appreciate your interest in my work and would like to record any comments you might like to make.
This one is an impression of the space shuttle Columbia in flight. It is what I call an arabesque — a design in my particular calligraphic style.
Last evening I thought of presenting it to you. I would like it to become part of your personal library. I feel it will have an especially meaningful relationship to you as an explorer of the universe.

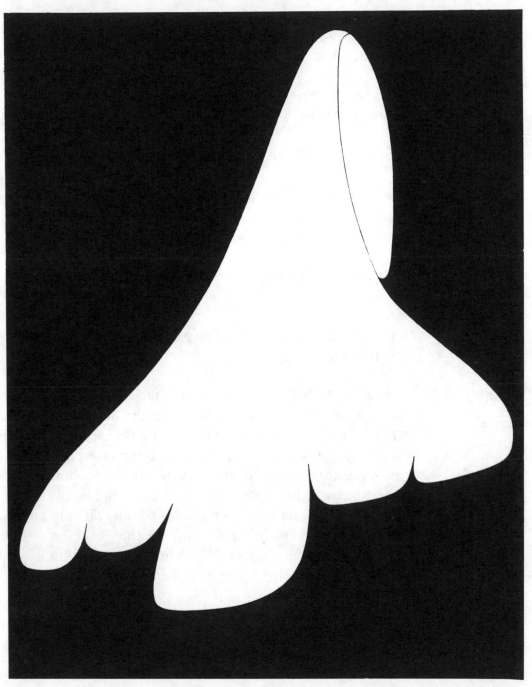

*"COLUMBIA: Arabesque 3"* © 1982 Anwar Dil. 22" × 30".

FULLER           Thank you. It's beautiful.
I would like it to go where it should go — to my place in Philadelphia. I am very grateful, sir.

DIL               This second one is the calligraph "Al-Hajar," the Arabic word for "The Stone."

FULLER           The fact is that this is more you than your "Columbia."

DIL               I would agree. It is a calligraph — a moment of togetherness of the sound, meaning and form of a word that is part of the basic vocabulary of human language.

FULLER           It is also much more you. This is the one I would really like to have from you.

DIL               All right, I am very pleased to present it to you in place of "Columbia."

FULLER           I would like you to write on a little card the following statement which we could frame with the calligraph:
It is a superb picture of what man calls stone, because stones are not solid, and stones are the consequence of atoms intermoving at various proximities, but never intertouching. I feel here the motions of the atoms. I feel it is a superb picture of what man has mistakenly called solid. And I take that *alif* to be me the observer — the observed and the observer. With me observing that which is not solid, which people mistakenly thought was solid.

*"AL-HAJAR: Calligraph 189." © 1982 Anwar Dil. 22" × 26".*
*The original is in Dr. Buckminster Fuller's Personal Collection at the Buck-
minster Fuller Institute, Philadelphia.*

*"NOAH: Calligraph 203." © 1982 Anwar Dil. 40" × 26".*

DIL

Here is my calligraph of "Noah." Last evening I did not understand what you said about it.

FULLER

I said Noah in the ancient Hebraic is Naga, the name for the sea serpent, the god of the sea which goes back before Poseidon and Neptune, the Greek and Roman gods of the sea. From most ancient times, sea people from around the world have put Naga on the prows of their ships.

I see there the boat. I see the boat with the mast and the sails all set. I see Naga as the boat, and Noah with Noah's ark, and all those things immediately together. It is very clearly the boat, a very beautiful boat. Look at it, there is a hull at the bottom and there are the sails. The mast and the sails, they are all there.

*"BISMILLAH: Calligraph 141."* © *1980 Anwar Dil. 22" × 30".*
*The original is in the collection of Mr. Asif Shakeel Ahmad, San Pedro, California.*

*"AL-JALEEL: Calligraph 150."* © *1980 Anwar Dil. 20" × 25".*

FULLER      That one is lovely.

DIL         "Tahira." You were especially interested in it last eve-
            ning. Tahira means "The Pure or Noble Woman."
            In doing this calligraph I had in mind Qurratul Ain Tahi-
            ra, a nineteenth-century mystic poet of Iran.

            *Lines from* the Song of Tahira

            Like the zephyr I have roamed
                that I may behold your face,
            From door to door, house to house,
                lane by lane, street by street.
            — Qurratul 'Ain Tahira's "Nawa-e-Tahira"

FULLER      See how much she is like a boat. She is a boat. She has a
            mast, and sails, and all. And she has something inside of
            her. As I said, all boats are female, because they have a
            hold, and you really see the child in her womb, there. See,
            right in the middle. She is a boat, she has a womb, and
            sails. And she has the moon and stars that guide your way
            by navigation. All those things are in there.

DIL         Dr. Fuller, you have made some very penetrating com-
            ments on my work that I have not heard anyone else
            make so far.

FULLER      I am sure nobody has said what I did. What I have is what
            I talked about earlier: aesthetics — my intuition in aes-
            thetics, my memory of experiences. I am a generalizer
            and I am looking for the generalized laws, and I am find-
            ing the generalized laws here, that is what I am describ-
            ing.

146

*"TAHIRA: Calligraph 198."* © 1982 Anwar Dil. 42" × 30".

My medium is pure form and I work with the interplay of positive and negative elements. Through the interaction of the basic opposition of black and white forms I seek to discover the *Cosmic Unity in Variety* and the incredible simplicity and elegance inherent in the Universe.

I am reminded here of a passage in Martin Buber's *I and Thou*: "This is the eternal origin of art that a human being confronts a form that wants to become a work through him. Not a figment of his soul but something that appears to the soul and demands the soul's creative power. What is required is a deed that a man does with his whole being: if he commits it and speaks with his being the basic word to the form that appears, then the creative power is released and the work comes into being." I feel that Buber wrote these lines to express the kind of challenge I face in doing my calligraphs.

I would like to share with you a few thoughts on calligraphic art, in the context of our discussion. For me, calligraphic art is far more comprehensive and inclusive in scope than the more traditionally-held view of calligraphy as good penmanship. The best of Chinese *Shu fa,* Islamic *Khattati,* Japanese *Shodo* and other traditions put calligraphic art at the intersection of all arts and sciences, including painting, poetry, music, architecture, mathematics, astrophysics, philosophy, mysticism and religion. The simple act of dividing a circle or a rectangle with a straight or curved line has the potential to create spatial forms that have beautiful and mysterious relationships with one another, as well as with the original form. Inspired by creative impulse associated with the sound, the meaning or the graphic form of a word, the mind of a calligraphic artist, working with simple forms, starts its artis-

*"YA HAFEEZ: Calligraph 138." © 1980 Anwar Dil. 20" × 25".*
*The original is in the artist's personal collection.*

tic exploration. In this process, individual letters and characters are linked together in innovative patterns. When the artist experiences a certain flow of vitality from a calligraph, very often he has discovered a form that is also full of abstract and symbolic beauty in the context of the word he has written.

For me, the creation of a calligraph is a deeply stirring experience — a moment of inner illumination. In this process I feel myself a witness to the beauty and power of the WORD. I derive inspiration from the WORD in its varied forms as manifested in the Universe, especially the names of men and women of excellence in history, and the qualities humans have attributed to God.

I aspire, through my calligraphs, to leave life a little more beautiful than when I came upon it.

"*ALIF LAAM MEEM: Calligraph 177.*" © 1981 Anwar Dil. 25$^1/_2''$ × 33$^1/_2''$. *The original is in the collection of Lalolagi Heini Forsyth and Dr. Mrs. Claudia Forsyth, Apia, Western Samoa.*

*"UMAR: Calligraph 154"* © *1980 Anwar Dil.* $25^{1}/_{2}''$ × *34".*
*The original is in the collection of Dr. John Efthimiou, Athens, Greece.*

*"ILAH: Calligraph 146." © 1980 Anwar Dil. 22" × 25".*
*The original is in the collection of Mr. Antony di Gesù, La Jolla, California.*

*"AL-TAUBA: Calligraph 205."* © 1982 Anwar Dil. 30″ × 40″.
*The original is in the Conference Room of Farukhi and Company, World Trade Center, Los Angeles.*

| | |
|---|---|
| FULLER | Where were you born? |
| DIL | I was born in Jullundur in the Punjab province in India. |
| FULLER | So you were born about 180 degrees around the world from me. |
| DIL | That's right. I was born in 1928, the year humans discovered the existence of a galaxy other than our Milky Way.<br>I have a poem I wrote last year that might interest you. |

*Dil's poem*

### Mine is the Light of a Distant Star

Mine is the light of a distant star.

It is there
> for you
> if only you look for it!

It does not dazzle
> as fireworks do, —
> the glory of a moment.

It is more like the light
> of Gandhara long ago,
> of men like Chanakya of Takshila.

It is there
> in the depths of your being
> the light of a distant star
> if only you look for it!

San Diego, California, March 22, 1981

154

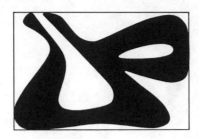

*"Ṣ (Ṣwaad): Calligraph 183." © 1981 Anwar Dil. 26″ × 40″.*
*The original is in the University of Mysore, Mysore, India.*

FULLER

*Fuller's inscription to Dil*

(Presenting an inscribed copy of his book, *Critical Path*[38]):

To Anwar Dil
On the day in which
he asked me what seems
to me to be
the right questions
to which I hope
that God inspired me
to give the nearest to right
answers
now to be had
and given.

DIL

Thank you so much.
You have added something here too.

FULLER

*(reading)*:
Anwar Dil, from Jullundur, Punjab, India, and
Buckminster Fuller, from Milton, Massachusetts, USA
meet in San Diego, California
December 4, 1982

*"ALI: Calligraph 145"* © *1980 Anwar Dil. 25$^1$/$_2$" × 34".*
*The original is in the Conference Room of the Embassy of Pakistan, New Delhi.*

# Epilogue

by Buckminster Fuller

*In 1889, six years before I was born, Rudyard Kipling wrote:*

*Oh, East is East, and West is West, and
  never the twain shall meet,
Till Earth and Sky stand presently at
  God's great Judgement Seat.*

*My co-author, Anwar Dil, born in Jullundur, Punjab, and I, Buckminster Fuller, born in Milton, Massachusetts, 180 degrees of both latitude and longitude apart, could not be more realistically representative of East and West. And in this book we meet and discuss the meeting of world-around minds. Once again, Kipling demonstrates the poet's extraordinary prophetic insight.*
*We and all our fellow Earthian humans are now hovering twixt mass entry into heaven versus continuance aboard our now-total-humanity-annihilating atomic-bomb-mounted Planet Earth. We are presently standing at "God's great Judgement Seat."*
*Whether humanity is to continue and comprehensively prosper on Spaceship Earth depends entirely on the integrity of human individuals and not on political and economic systems.*
*The cosmic question has been asked: Are humans a worthwhile-to-Universe invention?*
*When it is incontrovertibly established that, within the available lifetime to correct it, there exists an insurmountable condition of inadequacy of life support for all humans present, and when there is clear evidence that some of those present are incurably diseased and praying for termination of their lives, then the head of a healthy and unself-*

157

*ish family might with integrity adopt a selfish survival stra-
tegy for all those dependent on him or her.*

*We know that our spaceship Earth is approximately four
billion years old. We know that only within the last three
million of these four billion years have humans been
aboard our spaceship-planet.*

*We know something about human activity aboard Space-
ship Earth with documentable accuracy for only the last
eight thousand years.*

*Until only two hundred years ago, humanity was ninety-
eight percent illiterate. During the twentieth century, humanity has suddenly become sixty-five percent literate.*

*Two-and-three-quarters billion humans are now in on the
critical information. That is, there are now more literate,
informed people than all the humans on our planet eighty
years ago.*

*Many times in the eight thousand years of known history
lethal inadequacy of life support has existed in many areas
of Spaceship Earth's inhabited surface.*

*Because of these facts, evolution made selfishness impera-
tive in the struggle for existence. Only in the twentieth century did that start to change. During the twentieth century,
life expectancy has doubled as the prospects of fortunate
survival suddenly improved. Between the years 1900 and
1983, we have gone from less than one percent to the majority of all humanity enjoying a higher standard of living
than any potentate of 1900. The change has been brought
about by the invisible technology of a 99.999 percent invisible realm of electromagnetic, metallurgical and chemical reality.*

*In 1970, for the first time in history, it became technologi-
cally feasible to make all humanity a success. Because the
invisible technology can now produce so much high performance per each pound of material, erg of energy and
second of time invested, the invisible technology developed
the sustainable capability to take care of all the physical*

*needs and constructive pleasure of all humans aboard our Spaceship Earth and to do so within only ten years of design science revolution.*

*Comprehensive physical success for all can now be accomplished by converting all the materials and metals now invested in weaponry as well as the mass-manufacture machines and tools into producing only livingry. This sustainably-advanced standard of living for all can be attained while concurrently phasing out all use of fossil fuels and all electric energy generating by atomic reactors.*

*This being so, integrity can no longer tolerate selfishness.*

*Yesterday's condonable selfishness does not yet know that the conditions have changed. The challenge now facing the integrity of all Spaceship Earth's individuals is how to inform first themselves and then all the power structure leaders of the world that we now have the historically unprecedented option to "make it" for everyone and set about to exercise that option before the bombs go off.*

*Pacific Palisades, California*
*March 31, 1983*

*One of the last pictures of Buckminster Fuller in his Pacific Palisades home during the Fuller and Dil series of meetings © 1983 Kamran Anwar Dil.*

# *Appendix I*

Selections from Buckminster Fuller's
"How Little I Know" (1966)
(First published in the *Saturday Review*, November 12,
1966, pp. 29–31, 67–70. This version is from Fuller's
*And It Came to Pass — Not to Stay*. New York: Mac-
millan Publishing Co., 1976.)

"Tell me
In five thousand
Written words" –
(Equivalent, at my oral rate,
To three-quarters of an hour's discourse)
"What you have learned –
In your lifetime,"
Said Norman Cousins.
"That ought to be easy," said I.

Three weeks have gone by –

I recall that
Thirty-eight years ago
I invented a routine
Somewhat similar to
Muscle development
Accomplished through
A day-by-day lifting
Of progressively heavier weights.

But my new
Intellectual routine
Dealt with the weightless process
Of human thought development
Which subject is
Known to the scholars
As *epistemology*.

And I have learned
That such words as Epistemology
Stop most of humanity
From pursuing
Such important considerations
As the development
Of the thought processes.

So my new discipline
Was invented for dealing
Even with the ephemeral
Which word means
*Conceptual but weightless* –
As is for instance
The *concept* of *circularity*.

My new strategy required
That on successive days
I ask myself
A progressively larger
And more inclusive question
Which must be answered
Only in the terms of
Experience.

Hearsaids, beliefs, axioms,
Superstitions, guesses, opinions
Were and are
All excluded
As answer resources
For playing my particular
Intellectual development game.

However, when lacking
Any possible experience clues
I saw that it was ineffectual
To attempt to answer
Such questions as for instance

"Why I?"
Or
"Why . . .
Anything?"

And because it was my experience
That some individuals
Proved as persistently faithful
In reporting their experiences to me
As were my own senses
The rules of my game permitted
My inclusion of such individuals'
Directly reported experiences
In my inventory of experiences
For use in my progressively
Great and greater
Self-questioned answering.

In playing that game
I soon came
To what I assumed to be both
The largest askable and
The largest answerable
Question:
"What do you mean,"
I asked myself,
"By the word
Universe?
If you can't answer
In terms of
Direct experience
*You must desist*
*From the further use*
*Of the word* UNIVERSE
For, to you
It will have become
Meaningless!"

The 20th century physicists,
In defining physical Universe
As consisting only of energy,
Deliberately excluded metaphysical Universe —
Because the metaphysical
Consists only of imponderables,
Whereas the physical scientists
Deal only with ponderables —
Wherefore their physical Universe
Excluded for instance
All our thoughts —
Because thoughts are weightless —

But thoughts are experiences —
Wherefore I saw
That to be adequate
To the intuitively formulated
And experience-founded controls
Of my ever bigger
Question and answer routine,
My answering definition
Of UNIVERSE
Must be one which
*Embraced the combined*
*Metaphysical and physical*
*Components of* UNIVERSE.

Thus my self-formulating answer emerged,
And has persisted unshattered
By any subsequent challenges
From myself or others
As:
"By Universe I mean:
The aggregate of all humanity's
Consciously apprehended
And communicated
(To self or others)
*Experiences.*"

And later I discovered that
Eddington had said *"Science* is:
The conscientious attempt
To set in order
The facts of *Experience."*

And I also discovered
That Ernst Mach —
The great Viennese physicist,
Whose name is used
To designate flight velocity
In *speed of sound* increments,
Known as Mach numbers —
Said:
*"Physics* is:
*Experience*
Arranged in
*Most economical order."*

So I realized that
Both Eddington and Mach
Were seeking to put in *order*
The same "raw materials" —
*I. e. Experiences* —
With which to identify
Their special subsystems
Of UNIVERSE.

Wherefore I realized that
All the words in all dictionaries
Are the consequent tools
Of all men's conscious
And conscientious attempts
To communicate
All their experiences —
Which is of course
To communicate
Universe.

There are forty-three thousand current words
In the Concise Oxford Dictionary.
We don't know who invented them!
What an enormous, anonymous inheritance!
Shakespeare used ten thousand of them
With which to formulate
His complete "works."
It would take many more volumes
Than Shakespeare's to employ
The forty-three thousand —
Logically and cogently.

In a five thousand word article
I would probably have use for
Only one thousand.
Are forty-two thousand
Of these words
Superficial and extraneous
In reporting on
*What I have learned?*
I have learned that
You would think so
If you ever saw a magazine's
Space rewrite editor
At work on my work!
. . .

I'm not inclined to use
The word "Creativity"
In respect to human beings;
What is usually spoken of as creativity
Is really a unique and unprecedented
Human employment of *principles*
Which exist *a priori* in the Universe.

I think man is a very extra-ordinary
Part of the Universe

For he demonstrates unique capability
In the discovery and intellectual identification
Of the operative principles of Universe
— Which though unconsciously employed
Have not been hitherto differentiated,
Isolated out and understood
As being principles,
By other biological species.

Rejecting the word "creativity"
For use by any other than
The great intellectual integrity
Progressively disclosed as conceiving
Both comprehensively and anticipatorily
The complex interpatternings
Of reciprocal and transformative freedoms
In pure principle
Which apparently govern Universe
And constitute the verb god,
I go along with the 5,000-year-old
Philosophy of the Bhagavad-Gita
Which says "Action is the product
Of the qualities inherent in nature.
It is only the ignorant man,
Who, misled by personal egotism,
Says 'I am the doer.'"
I am most impressed
With the earliest recorded philosophic statements
By unknown individuals of India and China.
Through millenniums the philosophies
Have become progressively
Compromised and complicated.

I am an explorer, however,
Of the generalized design science principles
Which seemingly differentiate
Man from animal

And *mind* from *brain*.
The word "generalization"
As used in the *literary* sense,
Means "a very broad statement."
It suggests covering too much territory
— Too thinly to be sound.
The literary men say
"This is too general."

In the mathematical sense,
The meaning of generalization
Is quite different.
The mathematician or the physicist
Looks for principles which are
Persistently operative in nature,
Which will hold true in every special case.
If you can find principles
That hold true in every case,
Then you have discovered
What the scientist calls
A *generalized principle*.
The conscious detection of
Generalized principles which hold true
Under all conditions
And their abstraction from any and all
Special case experiences of the principles
— Is probably unique to humans.

By abstraction, I mean an idealized,
"Empty set" statement
Such as, for instance, one of my own!
— "Tension and compression are only coexistent"
— E. g., when you tense a rope
Its girth contracts — ergo compresses.
When you compress a sphere's polar axis,
Its equatorial girth expands and tenses,
It is inconceivable that a dog

Tugging at its leash at one time
And, compressing its teeth
On a bone at another time,
Should formulate consciously
The generalized
"Only coexistence of tension and compression,"
Though the dog is subconsciously coordinate
In tension-compression tactics.

To generalize further than
"Tension and compression are only coexistent,"
We may say that "plus and minus
Only coexist"
And generalize even further
By saying "Functions only coexist."
Then there is an even more powerful
And intellectually more exalted stage
Of generalization of principles
And that is the generalization
Of a complex of generalizations
− Such as − unity is plural and at minimum two
− Which combines the generalized law
Of the coexistence only of functions
With the theory of number.
In turn we discover the generalizations
Governing the associative powers
Of the nucleus and of the weak interactions
For the unity is two
Of the congruent, convex and concave spheres
As evidenceable in the generalized laws
Disclosed conceptually, arithmetically, and geometrically
In synergetics.

I am certain that what we speak of
As human morality
Is a form of tentative generalization
Of principles underlying

Special case experiences of human potentials,
Behaviors, actions, reactions and resultants.
Man has also the unique ability
To *employ* generalized principles
– Once recognized –
In a consciously selective variety
Of special case interrelationships.
The whole regenerative process
Of intellectual discovery
And specialized use of generalized principles
Is known as teleology.

Teleology embraces
The theory of communication,
Though as yet having special case limitations.
It is a hypothetical
Approach to pure, abstract generalization
To say that *teleology*
*Is only intuitively initiated by humans.*

Intuition alerts brain
To first apprehend
And then recognize
Each special case experience
Within some minimum number
Of special case recognitions.
Intuition alerts mind
To comprehend, and
Formulate conceptually
The abstract generalization
Of a principle recognized
As operative in all the special cases.
Intuition alerts brain to
The objectively employable generalized principle
In hitherto unexperienced special case
Circumstances inexplicably remote
From the earlier set of

Special case experiences within which
The generalized principles were first experienced
Before their generalization
Occurred in the mind.

Teleology — as part
Of communications theory
Relates to the pursuit of truth.
As entropy and antientropy.
It may be that
Communications theory
May be mathematically equated
With electrical
Transmission theory
Whereby the higher
The meaning or voltage
The more efficient
And longer distance
Communication attainable.

Based on experiments
With any *and* all systems,
The second law of thermodynamics
Predicts the inexorable energy loss
Known as ENTROPY.

Because the escaping energy
Does so diffusely,
In all directions,
Entropy is also known
Mathematically
As "The Law of Increase
Of the Random Element."

Before it had been discovered
By rigorous experimentation
That light has a *velocity*
It was erroneously assumed

To be "self-evident"
That light was instantaneous —
That all stars in the sky
Were "right there now"
In exact geometrical pattern,
Being seen instantaneously
And simultaneously
By all who looked their way.

But since Michelson's measurement
Of light's speed
We have learned that
The light from the Sun,
Our nearest star,
Takes eight minutes
To reach us here on Earth.
From our next nearest star
Light takes two years
To reach our planet Earth.
And other stars
Are so far away
Their light takes millions
Of years and more
To reach us.

Assuming instant-Universe
Classical Newtonian science
Also assumed that Universe
Must be an instant system —
A simultaneous unit machine,
In which every part
Must be affecting
Every other part,
In varying degrees
But in simultaneous unity.
They assumed also that the
Unit and simultaneous universe

Must of course obey
The great second law
Of thermodynamics
Whose, inexorable,
Entropic energy loss
Required self-dissipation
And ultimately utter
Self-annihilation
Of Universe.
"Running down" they called it
Wherever "down" may be.

Though light's speed
Of seven hundred million miles per hour
Is *fast*
It isn't anywhere nearly as fast
As "instant" −
Which means reaching anywhere
"In no time at all."

Ergo, the Einsteinians
Instituted experiments
To ascertain the behavioral characteristics
Of a physical universe comprised
Of only partially overlapping,
Progressively intertransforming,
Nonsimultaneous, energy events.

The Einsteinian Era scientists' experiments
Showed that entropic energies
Accomplished their disassociations *here*
Only through associations *there* −
That is by regrouping elsewhere.
Thus early 20th-century scientists
Found the intertransformative
Energy quanta transactions,
To be eventually,

But not always immediately,
One hundred percent accountable.

As a consequence of
The Einsteinians' experiments
The eighteenth and nineteenth centuries'
Concept of a continually
Self-dissipating universe
Had to be abandoned
And in its place was established
The, experimentally required,
Law of Conservation of Energy
Which states that energy
May be neither created nor lost;
Ergo the energetic Universe
Is the minimum,
But nonsimultaneously realized,
Energy exchanging system,
Which is to say
That physical Universe,
As experimentally demonstrated
Is the minimum and only
Perpetual motion process,
Which as an aggregate of finite,
Dissimilar and nonsimultaneous
Energy events
Is in itself
Sum totally finite.

All the foregoing
Dissipates the foundations
Of the Newtonian world's
Cosmogony and economics
Which assumed
That a "running down world"
Suggested the prudence
Of saving, conserving and hoarding;

And that those who spent
Were fools who would perish
As resources dwindled.

Though entropically irreversible
Every action
Has its reaction and resultant,
And every nuclear component
Has its positive or negative
Behavioral opposite
Which is however
Not its mirror image.

And the irreversible situations
Give an evolutionary direction
To otherwise stalemated
Conditions of physical Universe.

For instance it is discovered
That wealth, whatever else it may be,
Cannot alter an iota of yesterday
And can alter only
The present and forward
Metabolic regeneration
Conditions of humanity.

Song of the Dead
And the Quick —
Newton was a noun
And Einstein is a verb.
Einstein's norm makes Newton's norm
INSTANT UNIVERSE,
Absurd.
"A body persists
In a state of rest
Or —
Except as affected —"
Thus grave stones are erected!

Nonsimultaneous, physical Universe
Is Energy; and
"Energy equals mass
Times the second power
Of the speed of light."
No exceptions!
Fission verified Einstein's hypothesis —
Change is normal
Thank you Albert!

Irreversible verse.
Einstein's intellect
Defined *energy* as $E = mc^2$
*Energy* cannot define *intellect*.
Intellect the *metaphysical*
Is comprehensive to
Energy the *physical*.
While Universe is *finite*
Energy is *definite*
Because definable
Energy is XY.
Intellect is O.
The wealth of Earthians
Is irreversible.
Wealth cannot alter yesterday's experience.
It can only alter today's and tomorrow's experiences.
It can buy
Forward time in which intellect
May scientifically explore for
The orderly interrelationships
Disclosed in yesterday's experiences
Which can be employed by intellect
To forecast
Anticipatory and orderly rearrangements of tomorrow
By technological transformations
Of the physical energy environments,
Events and circumstances.

Wealth is the organized and operative
Tools and energy capability
To sustain man's forward metabolic regeneration;
To physically protect him;
To increase his knowledge
And degrees of freedom
While decreasing his interfrustrations.
Solo wealth is to commonwealth
As X is to $X^4$.
Wealth is: *Energy compounded*
*With intellect's know-how.*

Every time man uses his *know-how*
His experience increases
And his intellectual advantage
Automatically increases.
Because of its *conservation*
Energy cannot decrease.
Know-how can only increase.
It is therefore scientifically clear
That: − wealth which combines
Energy and intellect
Can *only increase,* and that wealth can
Increase *only with use*
And that wealth increases
As fast as it is used.
The faster − the more!

Wealth is accountable as
The inanimate energies shunted
Onto the ends of industrial levers
Whose physical capability is
Stateable in forward, automated,
Man days of travel miles
With first class comprehensive services
Including food, lodging, clothing,
Amusements, communication, information

And medical services
Based on the average physical experiences
Of a top civil service rating's
World travel involvements.

Has man a function
In Universe?

In dynamical balance
With the inside-outing,
*Expanding universe*
Of radiant stars,
Man witnesses
Radiantly dormant Earth as
A collecting or outside-inning,
*Contracting phase,* of Universe.
Earth receives and stores,
A continually increasing inventory
Of sun and star emanating radiation
In its lethal-energy-concentrates
Sifting, sorting and accumulating
Spherical Van Allen belts.

In addition to the Van Allen belts
The succession of Earth's concentric
Spherical mantles, e. g.,
The ionosphere, troposphere *et al.,*
Constitute an extraordinary series
Of discrete filters for
The random-to-orderly sorting,
Shunting, partially accumulating
And final inwardly forwarding
Of the benign radiation residues
To the biosphere stage
Of Earth's continual and orderly
Processing of its discrete share
Of the expanding-Universe-propagated
Energy income receipts.

Earth also receives daily
Additional thousands of tons
Of expanding-Universe-dispatched
Stardust.
This concentration around Earth's surface
Of the Universe-deposited dust
Apparently consists of 91 of the
92 regeneratively patterning
Chemical elements
In approximately the same systematic order
Of relative abundance of those elements
As the relative abundance
Of those same elements
As they are found to occur
In the thus far inventoried
Reaches of Universe.
The biological life on earth
Is inherently antientropic
For it negotiates the chemical sorting
Out of the Earth's crust's
Chemical elements inventory
And rearranges the atoms
In elegantly ordered
Molecular compound patternings.
Of all the biological antientropics,
I. e. random-to-orderly arrangers,
Man's intellect is by much
The most active, exquisite and effective agent
Thus far in evidence in Universe.
Through intellect, man constantly succeeds
In inventing technological means
Of doing ever more orderly
I. e., more efficient,
"Better sorted-out,"
Local Universe, energy tasks
With ever less units of investments

Of the (what may be *only apparently*),
*"Randomly" occurring*
Resources of energy,
As atomic matter,
Or *energy* as *channeled electromagnetics.*

To guarantee
All of life's
Antientropic functioning,
Intellectual integrity Universe
Which has designedly arranged the great game
Has also arranged that mankind,
Like all the other living species,
Has its ultra-shortsighted,
Built-in, "desire" drives,
Its romantic conception ambitions
And protectively colored self deceits,
As well as its longer distance "needs,"
All of which cause each species
To pursue its particular "honey"
With its particular rose-colored glasses,
As does the bumblebee
Which at the same time
Inadvertently and unconsciously performs
Myriads of other tasks,
Designed with fabulous
Scientific capability by nature,
Which inadvertent interco-ordinate tasks
Unknown to the separate creature species
Are all essential to realization
Of the regenerative continuance
Of the much larger
Survival support conditions
For the generalized
Ecological system of "all life."

It is part of
The comprehensively anticipating,
Design science of life
That the bumblebee's self-unviewed,
Unwitting, bumbling tail
Bumps into and knocks off male pollen,
Which it later
And again inadvertently,
Knocks off upon the female botanical organs,
Thus unconsciously participating in
A vastly complex ecological interaction
Of the many energy processing
Bio-chemical "gears"
Of the total life system
Dynamically constituted by
All the living species.
The myriad inadvertencies
Of all the living species
Have sum totally provided
A metabolically sustaining
And regenerative topsoil process
Which — it is realized now,
But only by
Our retrospectively gained knowledge —
Has kept man
Regeneratively alive on Earth
For at least two million years,
While ever improving
His physical survival advantages
And increasing his longevity.

This vast "game playing" of life
Has also indirectly occasioned
Not only the regenerative multiplication
Of human beings,

But also a progressively increasing
Percentage who survive in conditions
Of ever improving
Physical advantage.

I think man is very properly concerned
About that which he does not understand.
I don't think that it is the machine per se
That bothers man;
It is just not understanding
Anything
That disturbs him.
When an accident bares
Portions of human organs
Familiar only to doctors,
Those organs look foreign
And frightening to people.
Stick your tongue way out
Before a mirror.
It is a strange looking device.
If existing originally and
Transcendentally as psyches only,
Individuals had to choose,
And assemble their own sets
Of organic parts,
Having been assured of mortal incarnation
And of mortal "honey chasing" experiences
But only after successful selection
And completion of the assembly —
And were endowed — as psyches —
Only with an aesthetic
Sense of selectivity,
Being devoid of any understanding
Of either the separate or integrated
Functions of those parts —
No humans would merger

Those co-operatively functioning parts
Into mortal beings
For no part of the "guts"
Would be chosen.
Nature had to skin over the regenerative
Chemistry and physics controls,
With an aesthetically intriguing,
Pseudo-static, sculptural baby doll unity
In order to trick the immortal psyches
Into the problem-beset,
Temporary occupation
Of such humid process regenerative machines
As those of the humans.

I have learned
That man knows little
And thinks he knows a lot.
. . .
I am the most unlearned man I know.
I don't know anyone
Who has learned
How little one knows
As have I.
But that does not belittle
The little I seem to know,
And I have confidence
In the importance of remembering
How little we know
And of the possible significance
Of the fact that we prosper,
And at sometimes even enjoy
Life in Universe
Despite the designed-in littleness
That we have to "get by with."
. . .
What the astronomers rank as

The nearest bright star to Earth
Is "Rigel Kent"
Which is three hundred thousand times
Further away from earth than is the Sun.
It is easy to see a man
One third of a mile away and
We were surprised when young
To see a man
At that distance
Swinging a sledge
To drive a post into the ground
And to realize
That the sound of his maul
Hitting the post top
Registered in our brain
As reported through the ears
Four seconds later
Than had the visual news
Which "long since" had told us
That he had once more
Hit the post.
Through physical experiments
Performed by our scientists
We have learned that
The highest known velocity
Among physical phenomena
Is the speed of light and all radiation
Relayingly scanned by nerve lines
To our brain's television conceptualizing
Through the optics of our eyes.

Because the speed of light
Is approximately 186,000 miles per second,
And the Moon is
About twice that distance
Away from Earth.

If we had a large mirror on the Moon,
And we flashed a powerful
Light toward the Moon
It would take four seconds
For the light to be reflected back
To our eyes.
That is, the light takes
Two seconds to get to the Moon
And two more seconds
To return to Earth.
And the overall four seconds lag
Of the visual report
Is the same time lag as that in
Our childhood realized lag
Of the *sound report*
Behind the *visual report*
Of the post-sledging event.
Because the light coming to Earth
From the Moon
Takes two seconds to make the trip,
And because the light
Coming to Earth from the Sun
Takes eight and one-half minutes,
And because the light coming to us from Rigel Kent
Takes four and one-half years,
We all see a live show
Taking place in the sky
Four and one-half
Years ago.

And as we gaze around
The starry heavens
We see right now
Live shows of "yesterdays"
Ranging from millions to sextillions of years ago,
As we look at the stars

We see all of history
Now alive.

It took only two million years and
Four and one-half billion human babies
To establish a human survival beachhead
Aboard the little
Eight-thousand-mile-diameter
Spherical Spaceship EARTH
Whereby life could successfully realize
Its highest known potential life span
Possibly to continue indefinitely
As one self-rejuvenation generation.
Few of the stars we look at,
Live-starring out there,
Are young enough
To witness
Those first human events
Taking place on Earth
Only two millions of years ago.

Since all the vital parts
Of human organisms
Have now become interchangeable,
And many of them
Have also become interchangeable
With inanimate mechanical parts,
And since human longevity
Is continually increasing
There is a good possibility
That humanity is developing
A continuous human
Who will persist in prime health
And youthful vigor.

With the lessening of need
To replenish the population
With fresh baby starts,

The built-in drives to procreate
Will lessen and be manifest in a proclivity
Of females to camouflage as male
And males to camouflage as female
Thus suppressing the procreative urge
By superficial antipathetic illusions,
While permitting and promoting
Procreatively innocuous sex companionships.

Despite their billionfold numbers
Babies and very young children
Soon after their arrival on earth
Have uttered and continue to utter
Spontaneous comments and questions —
Concerning life on Earth
And in Universe —
Which are so economical
And uniquely fresh
In viewpoint and formulation
As to be pure poetry
Apparently proving that
Poetry is inexhaustible;
To which their sophisticated
And surprised off-guard adult audience
Cliche unpoetically
"Oh how cute."

In the year 1964
The one hundred largest
Industrial giant corporations,
Born and reared
In the United States of America
Invested four out of five
Of their new plant and equipment
Expansion dollars
In production and service facilities
In world lands outside the U.S.A.

This trending to World identity only
Of the industrial giants
Held true also not only with thousands
Of lesser magnitude
U.S.A. and European born
Limited liability industrial organizations
But also with the Communist countries'
Giant industrial organizations.
Wherefore world industrialization trends swiftly —
And altogether transcendentally
To man's conscious planning —
Into an unitarily co-ordinate
World giant
With built-in automated,
Research fed,
Computer analyzed and selected,
Evolutionary self-improving
And self-transforming
Through alternatingly regenerated
Competitive precessioning
Of all the variable functions
Of general systems theory.


TRUTH
I have learned that truth
Is an omnipresent, omnidirectional,
Evolutionary awareness,
One of whose myriadly multiplying facets
Discloses that there are no "absolutes"
—No "ends in themselves" — no "things"
—Only transitionally transformative verbing.

It seems possible to me
That God may be recognizable
In man's limited intellection
Only as the weightless passion drive

Which inspires our progressive searching
For the — momentarily only —
And only most-truthful-thus-far-possible —
Comprehension of all the interconnections
Of all experiences.
It seems then to me
That the nearer we come to understanding,
The nearer we come to the
Orderly omni-interrelationships
Of all the weightless complex
Of all generalized principles
Which seem to be disclosed to us
As so important
As to be tentatively identified as God.
For it is the integratable interrelationships
Of all the generalized laws
Which apparently govern
The great verb "Universe"
Of the vastly greater
—Because comprehensively anticipatory —
Verb *intellecting*
Which verb of optimum understanding
May be "God".

It seems that Truth
Is progressive approximation
In which the relative fraction
Of our spontaneously tolerated *residual error*
*Constantly diminishes.*

This is a typical
Antientropy proclivity of man
—Entropy being the law
Of *increase of the random element.*

Heisenberg's indeterminism,
In which the act of measuring

Always alters the measured,
Would seem entropic were it not
For the experimentally realized knowledge
That the successive alterations
Of the observed
Diminish
As both our tooling and instrumentation
Continually improve;
Ergo intellection's effect
Upon measurement and the measured
Is a gap closing,
And the pursuit of more truthful comprehension
Is successfully antientropic.

Before Heisenberg, T. S. Eliot said,
"Examination of history alters history"
And Ezra Pound,
And even earlier poets,
Reported their discoveries
That in one way or another
The act of thinking alters thought itself.

When we ask ourself
"What have we learned?"
We feel at first
That the answer is "nothing."

But as soon as we say so
We recall exceptions.
For instance we have learned
To test experimentally
The axioms given to us
As "educational" springboards, and
We have found
That most of the "springboards"
Do not spring
And some never existed.

As for instance
Points, holes,
Solids, surfaces,
Straight lines, planes,
"Instantaneous," "simultaneous,"
Things, nouns,
"Up," "down," "at rest"
The words "artificial" and "failure"
Are all meaningless.

For what they aver
Is experimentally "non-existent."
If nature permits a formulation
It is natural.
If nature's laws of behavior
Do not permit formulation
The latter does not occur.
Whatever can be done
Is natural,
No matter how grotesque, boring,
Unfamiliar or unprecedented.
In the same way
Nature never "fails."
Nature complies with her own laws.
*Nature is the law.*
When man lacks understanding
Of nature's laws
And a man-contrived structure
Buckles unexpectedly,
It does not fail.
It only demonstrates that man
Did not understand
Nature's laws and behaviors.
Nothing failed.
Man's knowledge or estimating
Was inadequate.
. . .

The second law of thermodynamics —
Entropy — is also as we have learned
The law of increase of the Random Element
I. e., every system loses energy — but
Synergy means
Behavior of whole systems
Unpredicted by
The behavior of any separate part.

EN-ergy behaves entropically.
SYN-ergy behaves syntropically.
God is entropy
And God is syntropy,
God is synergy.
God is energy.
And God is always
A verb —
The verbing of
Integrity.

I assume that the *physical Universe is definite*
And the *metaphysical Universe is finite.*
What men have called infinite
I call finite
And what men called finite
I call definite — i.e., definitive.
By my philosophy
The finite, but imponderable
Metaphysical Universe
Embraces the definite,
Ponderable, physical Universe.
*Finite* is not unitarily conceptual.
*Definite* is unitarily conceptual.
I have mathematical proof
That the difference between the sums
Of all the angles around all the surface vertices

Of any conceptual, definitive physical system
And the finite but non-conceptual metaphysical universe
Is always 720 degrees
Or a difference of only one
*Definitive tetrahedron,*
Therefore, the combined
Physical and metaphysical Universe is finite.

You can't buy anything worthwhile
Like spontaneous *love* or *understanding*.
Though metaphysically finite
These are imponderables.

The absolute would be
Nontransformable, static and weighable.
Ergo, experimentally meaningless.
Infinity is only local
And occurs within definite systems,
As for instance
Following a great circle
Around a sphere
Which because of the fact
That lines —
Which occur experimentally
Only as energy vectors —
Cannot go through
The same point
At the same time —
Due to interference,
Which means also that lines
As curves
Cannot re-enter, or
"Join back into themselves,"
Therefore, the circling line
Can only wrap around
And over its earlier part —
As the knot-making

Sailor says it,
The circle when followed
Around and around
Results in a coil
Which is an endless scenario —
An asymmetric spiral,
Which may be followed experimentally
Only as long as intellect is interested.

Not being simultaneous
Universe cannot consist of one function.
Functions only coexist.
Universe while finite is not definable.
I can define many of its parts
But I cannot define simultaneously
The nonsimultaneously occurring
Aggregate of partially overlapping experiences
Whose total set of local scenario relationships
Constitutes the whole Universe
Though the latter as an aggregate of finites
Is finite.
All the words
In all the dictionaries, as noted before,
Represent all of humanity's attempts
To express the aggregate of experiences — Universe.
And while the dictionaries are finite
All the words
In all the dictionaries
Cannot be read simultaneously
And there is not one
Simultaneous sentence
Inherent and readable
In all the words.
In the same way
All the nonsimultaneous experiences
May not be conceived

And expressed as
A simultaneous system.
Ergo, there is no thinkable and logical
Simultaneous conception
Of nonsimultaneous Universe.

There is strong awareness
That we have been overproducing
The army of rigorously disciplined
Scientific, game playing, academic specialists
Who through hard work
And suppressed imagination
Earn their Ph. D.s
And automatic contracts
With prime contractors
At fifteen thousand dollars
Per year — and more —
Only to have their specialized field
Become obsolete and by-passed in five years,
By severely altered techniques, instruments
And exploratory stratagems.
Despite their honor grades
They prove not to be
The Natural Philosophers
And scientist-artists, implied by their Ph. D.s
But just deluxe quality
Technicians or mechanics.
And a myriad
Of emergency committees —
Multiplying swiftly
From one or two
Emergency Committees
Appointed by the President,
Have altogether discovered
That what the
Ph. D. scientists lack —

To adapt themselves to change
Has been officially pronounced to be
"Creativity,"
But to my thinking
They lack the unique capability of mind —
Which is the ability not only to generalize
And to integrate a complex
Of pure generalizations
But also to project teleologically —
With fundamental understanding —
In any special case direction.
Fundamental wisdom
Can readily identify any and all
Special case aspects within
The generalized whole
When listening
Sensitively to one's intuitions
By which alone
The generalized sub-subconscious integration
Of pattern cognition feedbacks
Are articulated.

Philip Morrison — Cornell's head
Of the department of nuclear physics —
Talks about what he calls
"Left-hand" and "right-hand" sciences.
Right-hand science deals in all the proven
Scientific formulas and experiments.
Left-hand science deals in
All of the as yet *unknown* or *unproven* —
That is: With all it is going to take
Intellectually, intuitively, speculatively, imaginatively
And even mystically
By inspired persistence
To open up the as yet unknown.
The great scientists were great

Because they were the ones
Who dealt successfully with the unknown.
All the "greats" were left-hand scientists.
Despite this historical patterning of the "greats"
We have government underwriting
Only the right-hand science,
Making it bigger and sharper,
Rather than *more inclusive* and *understanding*! —
For how could Congress justify
Appropriations of billions for dreams?
So the billions went only
For the swiftly obsoleting
Bigger, faster and more incisive
Modifications of yesterday's certainties,
By Ph. D. specialists
Guaranteed by the great
Institutes of Technology
To which the Congress
Allocated the training funds
As obviously "safe"
And exempt from political criticism;
Despite that scientific investigation
Had shown beyond doubt
That almost all of America's
Top performance scientists
Had been educated
In small, liberal arts colleges,
And that almost all
Of those top scientists
Attributed their success
To their good fortune
In having studied intimately
With a great inspiring teacher.
It woud be considered
Political madness
To risk charges of corruption

Through voting government funds
To any individual
Especially to "great inspiring teachers" —
"Crackpot longhairs!"
So it goes —
To hell with the facts
When re-election
To political office is at stake.

Everything that constitutes science
Is unteachable.

And we recall that
Eddington said: "Science
Is the earnest attempt
Of *individual initiative*
To set in order
The facts of experience."
Scientific routines for specialized technicians
And scientific formulas for their reference
Alone are teachable. Initiative is unteachable.

Because we have been governmentally fostering
Ony right-hand science and
Right-hand science to excess
The U.S.A. President's science advisor
Instituted last year (1965)
A new direction of search
For sources of so-called "creativity."
Financed by the National Academy of Sciences,
He asked New York University's art department
To bring together a representative group of
America's leading art educators and artists.
It was felt by the National Academy
That the art educators —
As those who dealt with

Most of the almost drop-outs
Who had been switched into art
As a "last resort" —
Were probably intimate
With the type of emerging youth
Who were allowed to remain
In a freer state of mind
— In the world of art —
Than would they have been
If disciplined rigorously
In sharp specialization by the sciences.
That meeting I thought fascinating
For it disclosed the artists as being
Individuals who develop powerful self-protection
Of their innate intellectual
And conceptual capability inheritance.
They often protect their innate capabilities
Through intuitively triggered poker-faced silence
Which in the elementary or high schools
Is interpreted as non-cooperative, mental inferiority,
Often causing early termination
Of their formal education.
I think the consensus
Of the New York University meeting
Was that individuals
Of original conceptual brilliance
Were most frequently
Detected, protected, and made to grow
By equally sensitive art teachers.
"Great teachers."
Which agrees elegantly
With the statements
Of the proven scientists
Regarding their own experiences.
Congressional appropriations committees
Please take notice!

To comprehend the integral of art and science
As an irrepressible, intuitive creative urgency —
As an artist's need to articulate —
Kepes at Massachusetts Institute of Technology
Made a beautiful demonstration.

He took hundreds of 8″ × 10″
Black-and-white photographs
Of modern paintings and mixed them thoroughly
Like shuffled cards
With photographs taken by scientists
Through microscopes or telescopes
Of all manner of natural phenomena
Sound waves, chromosomes and such.
The only way you can classify
Photographs with nothing recognizable in them
Is by your own spontaneous
Pattern classifications.
Group the mealy, the blotchy, the striped,
The swirly, the polka-dotted,
        and their sub-combinations.
The pattern classified groups
Of photographs were displayed.
The artists' work and the scientists'
Were indistinguishable.
Checking the back-mounted data, it was found
That the artist had frequently conceived
The imagined pattern before
The scientist found it in nature.
Science began to take
A new view of artists.

Loving mothers
Prohibit here and promote there —
Often in ways irrelevant or frustrating
To brain-coordinated genetic evolution,
Often suppressing

A child's profound contribution
Trying to emerge.
We have to look on our society
As we look on the biological world in general
Recognizing, for instance,
The extraordinary contributions
Of the fungi, the manures, the worms, *et al.* −
In the chemical reprocessing −
And fertility up-grading of the earth.
We must learn to think
Of the functions of the trees' roots
As being of equal importance
To the leaves' functions.
We tend to applaud
Only the flower and the fruit
Just as we applaud only the football player
Who makes the touchdown
And not the linemen
Who opened the way.

What society applauds as "creative"
Is often isolated
Out of an extraordinary set
Of co-equal evolutionary events,
Most of which are invisible.
Evolutionary "touchdowns" are unpredictable −
Sometimes centuries apart.
Who knows which child
    is to make the next breakthrough?
In the next decade society
Is going to be preoccupied with the child
Because through the behavioral sciences
And electrical exploration of the brain
We find that given the right environment
And thoughtful answers to its questions
*The child has everything it needs educationally*
*Right from birth.*

We have thought erroneously of education
As the mature wisdom
And over-brimming knowledge of the grownups
Injected by the discipline pump
Into the otherwise "empty" child's head.
Sometimes parents say "don't"
Because they want to protect the child
From getting into trouble.
At other times when they fail to say "no"
The child gets into trouble.
The child, frustrated, stops exploring.
It is possible to design environments
Within which the child will be
Neither frustrated nor hurt
Yet free to self-educate, spontaneously and fully
Without trespassing on others.
I have learned to undertake
Reform of the environment
And not to try to reform man.
*If we design the environment properly*
It will permit both child and adult to develop safely
And to behave logically.

Order is achieved through — positive and negative —
Magnitude and frequency controlled alteration
Of the successive steering angles.
We move by zigzagging control
From one phase of physical Universe evolution
    to another.
The rudder concept of social law is most apt.
The late Norbert Wiener chose the word *cybernetics*
Derived from Greek roots of "rudder"
Because Wiener, Shannon and others
    in communication theory
Were exploring human behaviors
And their brain-controlled "feedback," etc.,

As a basis for the design of computers —
And it became evident
That the human brain only waveringly
Steers man through constant change.

No sharp cleavage is found
Which identifies the boundary between life and non-life,
Between the heretofore so-called "animate"
    and "inanimate."

Viruses,
The smallest organized structures
Exhibiting "life,"
May be classified either
As inanimate or animate —
As crystalline or "cellular" forms.
This is the level also at which
The DNA-RNA genetic code serves as
An angle and frequency designed
Structural pattern integrity.
Such pattern integrities
Are strictly accountable
Only as mathematical principles
Pattern integrities are found
At all levels of structural organization in Universe.
The DNA-RNA is a specialized case
Of the generalized principle of pattern integrity
Found throughout life and non-life.
All pattern integrity design
Is controlled entirely and only by
Angle and frequency modulation.
The biological corpus
Is not strictly "animate" at any point.
Given that the "ordering"
Of the corpus design
Is accomplished through such codings as DNA-RNA
Which are exclusively angle and frequency modulation.

Then we may go on to suggest
That "life," as we customarily define it
Could be effected at a distance.
Precession is the effect
Of one moving system
Upon another moving system.
Precession always produces
Angular changes of the movements
Of the effected bodies and
At angles other than 180 degrees,
That is, the results are never
Continuance in a straight line.
Ergo all bodies of Universe
Are effecting the other bodies
In varying degrees
And all the intergravitational effects
Are precessionally angular modulations
And all the interradiation effects
Are frequency modulations.

The gravitational and radiation effects
Could modulate the DNA-RNA
Angle and frequency instructions
At astronomical remoteness —
Life could be "sent on."

Within the order of evolution as usually drawn
Life "occurred" as a series
Of fortuitous probabilities in the primeval sea.
It could have been sent or "radiated" there.
That is, the prime code
Or angle and frequency modulated signal
Could have been transmitted
From a remote stellar location.
It seems more likely
(In view of the continuous rediscovery of humans
As fully organized beings

At ever more remote historical periods)
That the inanimate structural pattern integrity,
Which we call human being,
Was a frequency modulated code message
Beamed at Earth from remote location.
Man as prime organizing
"Principle" construct pattern integrity
Was radiated here from the stars —
Not as primal cell, but as
A fully articulated high order being,
Possibly as the synergetic totality
Of all the gravitation
And radiation effects
Of all the stars
In our galaxy
And from all the adjacent galaxies
With some weak effects
And some strong effects
And from all time.
And pattern itself being weightless,
The life integrities are apparently
Inherently immortal.

You and I
Are essential functions
Of Universe
We are exquisite syntropy.

I'll be seeing you!
Forever.

# Appendix II

Buckminster Fuller's
"Preparing For A Small One-Town World" (1975).
(Fuller's statement on May 15, 1975, as a witness before
the U.S. Senate Committee on Foreign Relations on the
United Nations. Other witnesses at the hearings in-
cluded: Bruno Bitker, Chairman, Wisconsin Governor's
Commission on the United Nations; Seyom Brown,
Brookings Institution; Norman Cousins, Editor, *Saturday
Review*; John A. Scali, U.S. Representative to the United
Nations. From *The Congressional Record — Senate*, May
22, 1975.)

In my lifetime of 80 years I have seen a great deal of
change. I grew up in an era when 99% of humanity travelled only very locally on foot, horse, and bicycle and av-
eraged 1100 miles per year of local linear motion plus
300 miles per year of riding on horses or in vehicles.
The pre-airplane and radio world with 88% of humanity
consisting of Asia's 52%, Europe's 26%, Africa's 10%,
all very remote from the America's 12%. Seventy years
ago, it took three months to get to India. My last trip to
India, 1974, was quicker than either my first trip from
Boston to New York as a child, or my first trip after
World War I from New York City to Chicago on the then
blue ribbon New York Central Railway's "Twentieth
Century Limited." Now I reach India by telephone in a
couple of minutes. I find present world affairs inherently
integrated despite the hindering persistence of the 150
national sovereignties as our conditioned reflex heritage
from all of the previous milleniums of inherent separation
of interests. In 1961, three jet planes out-performed the
Queen Mary in one third the time for one half the price.
The oceans became obsolete as a means of getting humans from here to there. The era of water surface travel

stopped without people realizing what had happened. We have been hurled by evolution into a one-small-world-town within which average humans are travelling 11,000 miles annually — ten times their coverage of pre-World War I and many millions of worldians such as I cover 150,000 miles per year, and astronauts travel 3,000,000 miles per year.

The standard Mercator projection was developed for the world oriented to the ocean communication. All the transoceanic nations were connected only by ship. The "Roaring South Forties" latitudes Antarctic winds and waters' west-to-east whirl-around, swiftly interconnecting the Pacific, Atlantic, and Indian oceans south of Good Hope, the Horn, and New Zealand's South Island, and the ocean's trade winds altogether formed a pattern of most advantageous voyaging of which the world-around trading ships took advantage. The masters of the seas were those who controlled the Antarctic interocean whirl-around by maintaining naval bases at the southern tips of Africa, Australia, New Zealand, and South America, near to which bases all ships had to pass to get from ocean to ocean unseen and unnoticed to the 90% of humanity living in the Northern Hemisphere. The masters of those Antarctic Ocean integrated shipping lanes controlled the wealth making of our Earth. The Mercator projection was appropriate enough when people sailed around Earth's middle latitudes which it distorts the least, but it is obsolete in air-borne world traffic considerations. The Mercator ignores the poles and distorts the polar regions, showing Greenland three times bigger than Australia.

My Dymaxion map with the South Pole as its center presents an unfamiliar but most realistic picture of the British Empire's strategic mastery of World One — the pre-airplane and radio Earth. It shows Australia as the continent it is, four times as big as Greenland. With the Dymaxion projection you can see the whole world at once, with no visible distortion of the relative shape or size of any of the parts. If you show 100% of any data against this background, it will read properly, for my map's area and shape proportionality is uniform.

If you rearrange the pieces of the Dymaxion map with the North Pole at the center, you will see World Two, a one world island. That is the map of our present era. 85% of all the land in the world is north of the equator. Less than 10% of humanity lives south of the equator. 90% of humanity can reach each other via the shortest great circle air routes over the Pole without going near the Atlantic, Pacific, or Indian Oceans. The old east/west, north/south separations, with each nation looking out for itself, are no longer valid. The fragmentation of the world into nations that was logical yesterday, when men were inherently divided by the time and space, is no longer valid nor socio-economically tenable.

We have utter intimacy of communication, and willy-nilly, we have complete integration of the interests of all humanity.

I no longer think of underdeveloped and small nations that need help, and big rich ones that must help them. I see all mankind being integrated into one world pattern despite the still operative sovereign nationalities which in fact are functionally extinct, and their continued presence is the world's number one pollutant. Both the world's political powers and monetary powers have had to go supra-national. They leave only the individual human's passport control trapped in 150 national border controlled pens, subject to conscription, taxation, and the social cancer of non-thinking bureaucracy. The mobile young are beginning to live all around the world. As a half century's visiting professor at 420 universities around the world, I find that the natural tendency of students is to regard themselves as world citizens, which is what they are and want to be recognized as. Students from New Guinea and from Africa who go to Europe and America for training, want naturally to go back to their villages to help their people, but they are beginning to find that the village and the family at home want to become part of the greater world too. No doubt there will be a very long period of transition, but there has to be complete accommodation of this new way in which humanity is beginning to think and to live.

## Economic Revolutions

I was born in a society where 90% of the people had to live on farms to grow their own food. I was a grown man when we learned ways of getting the food into cans, and refrigerated transport to reach people anywhere. After World War I we learned to handle great farms mechanically, almost without human labor. But we have not changed our economic accounting systems which are all based on a seasonal agrarian economy, even though the year no longer has anything to do with the industrial cycle. An industrial generation in 22 years brought about the rate at which the average bulk of all metals are melted out of old uses to be formed into the new. Every time they are recycled the interim 22 year gain in technological know-how has increased so greatly that on an average the same tons of metal serve four times as many humans with vastly improved performance. This brought about an incredible transition, all unexpected by humanity between 1900 and 1975 where 52% of humanity is now enjoying a standard of living superior to that of any monarch of 1900 as their life expectancy also doubled within that time. The tasks to be done in our industrial economies may run into thirty, forty, or fifty year cycles. Both business leaders and politicians have to make either monetary or popularity "profits" within three years or they lose their jobs. People don't comprehend or tolerate undertaking of something that is going to take forty or fifty years to develop. The kind of permanent buildings we have were logical if humans stayed put on the land, but they are not doing so. Most of the 90% of humanity which before World War I was on the farm has come temporarily into the cities, hoping for employment and the good life. The cities were not designed to take care of them. Populations are continuing to shift only expediently from country to city, and city to mega-city with landlords reaping harvests of dollars at ever-escalating prices out of the entrapped population.

## Cities in the Twentieth Century

Men came to cities in the past because there were harbors and warehouses, and that was the place to find jobs, but the jobs have deployed out from the cities, as far as physical production and retail commerce goes. Big cities, instead of being warehouses and centers for the exchange of physical goods, are developing into metaphysical exchanges. For example, New York City's ocean docks are empty as are the surrounding railroad freight yards. Obsolete except as a convention and amusement city, New York is being taken over by the great universities, the United Nations, and the like, for the inter-change of ideas, or by wealth value exchanges like the banks and stock exchanges that deal in paper abstractions, bonds, stocks, money, and credit. The big cities are processing the metaphysical, and the physical is increasingly processed outside the cities.

## The Greatest Revolution

We are entered upon the greatest revolution in the history of humanity: either it is going to be a bloody revolution of trying vindictively to pull the top down in which everybody loses or a technological design science-revolution in which all humanity is elevated to higher standards of living than any have ever heretofore experienced.

It is not a matter of who is going to make the most money or political kudos, but how to make humanity a success. That is the challenge. There can be no compromise. We now know enough about how to make our world work to provide all humanity with the option of total sustainable physical success.

If we are going to be able to take care of humanity, we must find out how most economically and satisfactorily to control our environment.

The land building arts are 5000 years behind the ship building and aerospace ship design and production technology. What equipment do we need to do it? Humanity must achieve the success it was designed to be. But we are at the point where there could be a stillbirth. Nothing is so critical as birth, and whether the world survives birth into an entirely new world and universe relationship depends on our individual integrity, not on that of political representatives. We have enough technological know-how at our disposal to give everyone a decent life, and release humanity to do what it is supposed to be doing — that is, using our minds, accomplishing extraordinary things, not just coping with survival. You and I are given hunger so that we will be sure to take on fuel and regenerate our bodies; we are given a drive to procreate so that mankind will be regenerated; we are given brains with which to apprehend and recallably store information. We are also given minds with which to discover metaphysical principles. The function of mankind is to think, to discover and use principles. We are here to serve as local universe information harvesters and as local universe problem solvers employing human mind's unique access through science to some of the generalized principles governing eternally regenerative universe. We are going to have to exercise this responsibility within decades or perish.

# *Appendix III*

Buckminster Fuller's "Mistake Mystique" (1977).
(From *East West*, April 1977, pp. 26, 28−29.)

"What do you think is the greatest challenge facing young people today as they prepare to assume their caretakership of this world?" was the question recently asked of me by a midwest high school.

From my viewpoint, by far the greatest challenge facing the young people today is that of responding and conforming only to their own most delicately insistent intuitive awarenesses of what the truth seems to them to be as based on their own experiences and not on what others have interpreted to be the truth regarding events of which neither they nor others have experience-based knowledge.

This also means not yielding unthinkingly to "in" movements or to crowd psychology. This involves assessing thoughtfully one's own urges. It involves understanding but not being swayed by the spontaneous group spirit of youth. It involves thinking before acting in every instance. It involves eschewing all loyalties to other than the truth and love through which the cosmic integrity and absolute wisdom we identify inadequately by the name "God" speaks to each of us directly − and speaks only through our individual awareness of truth and our most spontaneous and powerful emotions of love and compassion.

The whole complex of omni-interaccommodative generalized principles thus far found by science to be governing all the behaviors of Universe altogether manifest an infallible wisdom's interconsiderate, unified design, ergo an a priori, intellectual integrity conceptioning, as well as a human intellect discoverability.

That is why youth's self-preparation for planetary care-takership involves commitment to comprehensive concern only with all humanity's welfaring; all the experimentally demonstrable, mathematically generalized principles thus far discovered by humans, and all the special case truths as we progressively discover them — the universally favorable synergetic consequences of which integrating commitments, unpredictable by any of those commitments when they are considered only separately, may well raise the curtain on a new and universally propitious era of humans in universe.

By cosmic designing wisdom we are all born naked, helpless for months, and though superbly equipped cerebrally, utterly lacking in experience, ergo utterly ignorant. We were also endowed with hunger, thirst, curiosity, and procreative urge. We were designed predominantly of water — which freezes, boils, and evaporates within a miniscule temperature range. The brain's information-apprehending, -storing, and -retrieving functions, as the control centers of the physical organisms employed by our metaphysical minds, were altogether designed to prosper initially only within those close thermal and other biospheric limits of planet Earth.

Under all the foregoing conditions, whatever humans have learned had to be learned as a consequence only of trial-and-error experience. Humans have learned only through mistakes. The billions of humans in history have had to make quadrillions of mistakes to have arrived at the state where we now have 150,000 common words to identify that many unique and only metaphysically comprehendible nuances of experience. The number of words in the dictionary will always multiply as we experience the progressive complex of cosmic episodes of scenario universe, making many new mistakes within the new set of unfamiliar circumstances. This provokes thoughtful reconsideration, and determination to avoid future mistake making under these latest given circumstances. This in turn occasions the inventing of more incisively effective word tools to cope with the newly familiar phenomena. Also by wisdom of the great design, humans have the capability to formulate and communicate from generation to generation their newly evolved thoughts regarding these lessons of greater experience which are only expressible through those new words and thus progressively to accumulate new knowledge, new viewpoints, and new wisdom, by sharing the exclusively self-discovered significance of the new nuances of thought.

Those quadrillions of mistakes were the price paid by humanity for its surprising competence as presently accrued synergetically, for the first time in history, to cope successfully on behalf of all humanity with all problems of physically healthy survival, enlightening growth, and initiative accommodation.

Chagrin and mortification caused by their progressively self-discovered quadrillions of errors would long ago have given humanity such an inferiority complex that it would have become too discouraged to continue with the life experience. To avoid such a proclivity, humans were designedly given pride, vanity, and inventive memory, which, all together, can and usually do incline us to self-deception.

Witnessing the mistakes of others, the preconditioned crowd, reflexing, says, "Why did that individual make such a stupid mistake? We knew the answer all the time." So effective has been the nonthinking, group deceit of humanity that it now says, "Nobody should make mistakes," and punishes people for making mistakes. In love-generated fear for their children's future life in days beyond their own survival, parents train their children to avoid making mistakes lest they be put at a social disadvantage.

Thus humanity has developed a comprehensive, mutual self-deception and has made the total mistake of not perceiving that realistic thinking accrues only after mistake making, which is the cosmic wisdom's most cogent way of teaching each of us how to carry on. It is only at the moment of humans' realistic admission to selves of having made a mistake that they are closest to that mysterious integrity governing the universe. Only then are humans able to free themselves of the misconceptions that have brought about their mistakes. With the misconceptions out of the way, they have their first view of the truth and immediately subsequent insights into the significance of the misconception as usually fostered by their pride and vanity, or by unthinking popular accord.

The courage to adhere to the truth as we learn it involves, then, the courage to face ourselves with the clear admission of all the mistakes we have made. Mistakes are sins only when not admitted. Etymologically, sin means *omission* where *admission* should have occurred. An angle is a *sinus,* an opening, a break in a circle, an omission in the ever-evolving integrity of the whole human individual. Trigonometrically, the sine of an angle is the ratio of the length of the side facing the central angle considered, as ratioed to the length of the radius of the circle.

Human beings were given a left foot and a right foot to make a mistake first to the left, then to the right, left again, and repeat. Between the over-controlled steering impulses, humans inadvertently attain the between-the-two desired direction of advance. This is not only the way humans work — it is the way the universe works. This is why physics has found no straight lines; it has found a physical universe consisting only of waves.

*Cybernetics,* the Greek word for the steering of a boat, was first employed by Norbert Weiner to identify the human process of gaining and employing information. When a rudder of a ship of either the air or sea is angled to one side or the other of the ship's keel line, the ship's hull begins to rotate around its pivot point. The momentum of that pivoting tends to keep rotating the ship beyond the helmsman's intention. He or she therefore has to "meet" that course-altering momentum whose momentum in turn has again to be met. It is impossible to eliminate altogether the ship's course realterations. It is possible only to reduce the degree of successive angular errors by ever more sensitive, frequent, and gentle corrections. That's what good helmsmen or good airplane pilots do.

Norbert Weiner next invented the word *feedback* to identify discovery of all such biased errors and the mechanism of their overcorrections. In such angular error correction systems (as governed, for instance, by the true north-holding direction sustained by the powerful angular momentum of gyroscopes which are connected by delicate hydro- or electrically actuated servo-mechanisms to the powerful rudder-steering motors), the magnitude of rightward and leftward veering is significantly reduced. Such automated steering is accomplished only by minimizing angular errors, and not by eliminating them, and certainly not by pretending they do not exist. Gyro-steering produces a wavilinear course, with errors of much higher frequency of alternate correction and of much lesser wave depth than those made by the human handling of the rudder.

All designing of the universe is accomplished only through such alternating angle and frequency modulation. The DNA-RNA codes found within the protein shells of viruses which govern the designing of all known terrestrial species of biological organisms consist only of angle and frequency modulating instructions.

At present, teachers, professors, and their helpers go over the students' examinations, looking for errors. They usually ratio the percentage of error to the percentage of correctly remembered concepts to which the students have been exposed. I suggest that the teaching world alter this practice and adopt the requirement that all students periodically submit a written account of all the mistakes they have made, not only regarding the course subject, but in their self-discipline during the term, while also recording what they have learned from the recognition that they have made the mistakes; the reports should summarize what it is they have really learned, not only in their courses, but on their own intuition and initiative. I suggest, then, that the faculty be marked as well as the students on a basis of their effectiveness in helping the students to learn anything important about any subject — doing so by nature's prescribed trial and error leverage. The more mistakes the students discover, the higher their grade.

The greatest lesson that nature is now trying to teach humanity is that when the bumblebee goes after its honey, it inadvertently pollinizes the vegetation, which pollinization, accomplished at 90 degrees to the bumblebee's aimed activity, constitutes part of the link-up of the great ecological regeneration of the capability of terrestrial vegetation to impound upon our planet enough of the sun's radiation energy to support regeneration of life on our planet, possibly in turn to support the continuation of humans, whose minds are uniquely capable of discovering some of the eternal laws of universe and thereby to serve as local universe problem solvers in local maintenance of the integrity of eternal regeneration of the universe.

In the same indirect way, humanity is at present being taught by nature that its armament making as a way to make a living for itself is inadvertently producing side effects of gained knowledge of how to do ever more with ever less and how, therewith, to render all the resources on earth capable of successful support of all humanity.

The big lesson, then, is called *precession*. The 90 degree precessional resultants of the interaction of forces in Universe teach humanity that what it thought were the side effects are the main effects, and vice versa.

What, then, are the side effects of knowledge gained by students as a consequence of the teacher's attempt to focus the students' attention on single subjects? It can be that all the categories of informational educational systems' studies are like the honey-bearing flowers, and that the really important consequence of the educational system is not the special case information that the students gain from any special subject, but the side effects learning of the interrelatedness of all things — and thereby the individual personal discovery of an overall sense of the omnipresence and reliability of generalized principles governing the omnirelatedness — whereby, in turn, the individuals discover their own cosmic significance as co-functions of the "otherness," which co-functioning is first responsible to all others (not self), and to truth which is God, which embraces and permeates Scenario Universe.

The motto of Milton Academy, the Harvard preparatory school I attended, was "Dare to Be True." In the crowd psychology and mores of that pre-World War I period, the students interpreted this motto as a challenge rather than an admonition, ergo, as: "Dare to tell the truth as you see it and you'll find yourself in trouble. Better to learn how the story goes that everybody accepts and stick with that."

Ralph Waldo Emerson said, "Poetry means saying the most important things in the simplest way." I might have answered the school in a much more poetical way by quoting only the motto of 340-year-old Harvard University, "*Veritas*" (Vere-i-tas), meaning progressively minimizing the magnitude of our veering to one side or the other of the star by which we steer, whose pathway to us is delicately reflected on the sea of life, and along whose twinkling stepping-stone path we attempt to travel toward that which is God — toward truth so exquisite as to be dimensionless, yet from moment to moment so reinformative as to guarantee the integrity of eternally regenerative Scenario Universe.

*Veritas* — it will never be superseded.

# Appendix IV

Buckminster Fuller's "Integrity" (1982).
(From *The Review*, November/December 1982,
pp. 3–5.)

A very large number of Earthians, possibly the majority,
sense the increasing imminence of total extinction of humanity by the more than 50,000 poised-for-delivery
atomic bombs. Apparently no one of the $4\,^1/_2$ billion humans on our planet knows what to do about it, including
the world's most powerful political leaders.

Humans did not invent atoms. Humans discovered
atoms, together with some of the mathematically incisive
laws governing their behavior.

In 1928 humans discovered the existence of a galaxy other than our own Milky Way. Since then we have discovered 2 billion more galaxies, each averaging over 100 billion stars. Each star is an all-out chain-reacting atomic
energy plant.

Humans did not invent the gravity cohering the macrocosm and microcosm of eternally regenerative Universe.
Humans did not invent humans, nor the boiling and
freezing points of water. Humans are 60 percent water.
Humans did not invent the 92 regenerative chemical elements or the planet Earth with its unique biological life-
supporting and protecting conditions.

Humans did not invent the radiation received from our
atomic energy generator, the Sun, around which we designedly orbit at a distance of 92 million miles.

The farther away from its source, the less intense the radiation. With all the space of Universe to work with, nature found 92 million miles to be the minimum safe remoteness of biological protoplasm from atomic radiation
generators.

Humans did not invent the vast distance-spanning photo-synthetic process by which the vegetation on our planet can transceive the radiation from the 92-million-miles-away Sun and transform it into the hydrocarbon molecules structuring and nurturing all life on planet Earth.

Design is: both subjective and objective, exclusively intellectual, mathematical conceptioning of orderliness of interrelationships.

Since all the cosmic-scale inventing and designing is accomplishable only by intellect and it is not by the intellect of humans, it is obviously that of the eternal intellectual integrity we call God.

All living creatures including humans have always been designed to be born unclothed, utterly inexperienced, ergo absolutely ignorant. Driven by hunger, thirst, respiration, curiosity and instincts such as the reproductive urge, all creatures are forced to take speculative initiatives or to "follow the herd," else they perish.

Ecological life is designed to learn only by trial and error. Common to all creature experience is a cumulative inventory of only-by-trial-and-error-developed problem-solving reflexes.

Unique only to human experience is the fact that problem-solving leads not only to fresh "pastures," but sometimes to ever more intellectually challenging problems. These challenges sometimes prove to be new, more comprehensively advantaging to humanity, mathematically generalizable, cosmic design concepts.

Humans have had to make trillions of mistakes to acquire the little we have as yet learned.

The greatest mistake we have ever made is to assume that the supreme authority governing life and Universe is not God but is either luck or the dictum of the humanly constituted and armed most-powerful socioeconomic systems and religions. The combined human power structures — economic, religious, and political — have compounded this primary error by ruling that no one should make mistakes and punishing those who do. This deprives humans of their only-by-trial-and-error learning. The power structure's forbiddance of error-making has fostered cover-upping, self deceiving, egotism, false fronts, hypocrisy, legally enacted or decreed subterfuge, ethical codes and the economic rewarding of selfishness.

Selfishness has in turn fostered both individual and national bluffing and vastness of armaments. Thus we have come to the greatest of problems ever to confront humanity — What can the little individual human do about the supranational corporate power structures and their seemingly ungovernable capability to corrupt?

A successful U.S. presidency campaign requires a minimum of 50 million dollars, senatorships 20 million, representatives 2 million. Through big business's advertising-placement control of the most powerful media, money can buy and now has bought control of the U.S.A. political system once designed for democracy.

Without God, the little individual human can do nothing. Brains of all creatures, including humans, are always and only preoccupied in coordinating the information fed into the brain's imagination — image-ination — scenarioing center by the physical senses and the brain-remembered previous similar experience patterns and the previous reflexive responses.

Human mind alone has been given access to some of the eternal laws governing physical and metaphysical Universe, such as the laws of leverage, mechanical advantage, mathematics, chemistry, electricity, and the laws governing gravitational or magnetic interattractiveness as is manifested by the progressive terminal acceleration of Earthward traveling bodies or by the final "snap" together of two interapproached magnets.

Employing those principles first in weapons and subsequently in livingry, humans have been able to illumine the nights of all humanity with electricity and to intercommunicate with telephones and to integrate the daily lives of the remotest-from-one-another humans with the airplane.

As a consequence of human mind's solving problems with technology, within only the last three-fourths of a century of our multimillion of years' presence on planet Earth the technical design initiatives have succeeded in advancing the standard of living of the majority of humanity to a level unknown or undreamed of by any pre-20th century potentates.

Within only the last century, humanity has grown from 95 percent illiterate to 65 percent literate. Preponderantly illiterate humanity needed literate leaders. Now, preponderantly literate humanity is capable of self-instruction and self-determination in major degree.

Clearly humanity is being evolutionarily ejected ever more swiftly from all the yesteryears' group-womb of designedly permitted ignorance.

Regarding the power-structure-supported scriptures' legend of woman emanating from a man's rib, there is no sustaining experiential evidence.

Humanity now knows that only women can conceive, gestate, and bear both male and female humans. Women are the continuum of human life. Like the tension of gravity-cohering space-islanded galaxies, stars, planets, and atoms, women are continuous. Men are discontinuous space islands. Men, born forth only from the wombs of women, have the function of activating women's reproductivity.

The present evolutionary crisis of humans on planet Earth is that of a final examination for their continuance in Universe. It is not an examination of political, economic, or religious systems, but of the integrity of each and all individual humans' responsible thinking and unselfish response to the acceleration in evolution's evermore unprecedented events.

These evolutionary events are the disconnective events attendant upon the historic termination of all nations. We now have 163 national economic "blood clots" in our planetary production and distribution system. What is going on is the swift integration in a myriad of ways of all humanity not into a "united nations" but into a united space-planet people.

Always and only employing all the planet's physical and metaphysical resources only for all the people, this evolutionary trend of events will result in an almost immediately higher standard of living for all than has ever been experienced by anyone. The higher the standard of living, the lower the birth rate.

The population-stabilizing higher living standards will be accomplished through conversion of all the high technology now employed in weaponry production redirected into livingry production, blocked only by political party traditions and individually uncoped-with, obsoletely conditioned reflexes.

A few instances of persistent, misinformedly conditioned reflexes are: the failure popularly to recognize the now scientifically proven fact that there are no different races or classes of humans; or failure to recognize technological obsolescence of the world-around politically assumed Malthus-Darwin assumption of an inherent inadequacy of life support, ergo "survival only of the fittest"; or failure to ratify ERA, the Equal Rights (for women) Amendment, by the thus far in history most crossbred-world-peoples' democracy in the U.S.A.; or, with ample food production for all Earthians, the tolerating of marketing systems which result in 41,000 humans dying of starvation each and every one of the 365 days of each and every year.

Carelessly unchallenged persistence of a myriad of such misinformed brain reflexings of the masses will signal such lack of people's integrity as to call for the disqualification of humanity and its elimination by atomic holocaust.

You may feel helpless about stopping the bomb.

To you, the connection between the Equal Rights Amendment and the atomic holocaust may at first seem remote. I am confident that what I am saying is true. The holocaust can be prevented only by individual humans demonstrating uncompromising integrity in all matters, thus qualifying us for continuance in the semi-divine designing initiative bestowed upon us in the gift of our mind.

# Notes

1. Anthony Tucker's "An architect building on cosmic energy, not revenue meters." *The Guardian,* April 14, 1983, p. 17.

2. Edward Campbell's "Giant's vast warning for mankind." *Sunday Standard* (Glasgow Weekly), April 17, 1983.

3. Osgood Caruthers' "Khrushchev, at U.S. Fair Site, Impressed by Aluminum Dome." *The New York Times,* May 5, 1959, p. 1.

4. Adam Williams' "US inventor takes China by storm." *South China Morning Post* (Hong Kong), May 30, 1979, p. 1.

5. Text of "Opening Speech" by Prime Minister Shrimati Indira Gandhi at the Third Jawaharlal Nehru Memorial Lecture, New Delhi, 1969. (Buckminster Fuller Institute Archives, Philadelphia)

6. Letter of Mrs. Claire Booth Luce to the President of the United States of America, May 29, 1978. (Buckminster Fuller Institute Archives, Philadelphia)

7. Letter of Archibald MacLeish to the President of the United States of America, February 24, 1978. (Buckminster Fuller Institute Archives, Philadelphia)

8. Buckminster Fuller, *Intuition* (New York: Doubleday, 1972). Revised edition, Anchor Press, 1973; Second edition, Impact Publishers, San Luis Obispo, California, 1983.

9. Ezra Pound, *The Cantos of Ezra Pound* (New York: New Directions, 1970), p. 795−96.

10. Ibid., p. 802.

11. T. S. Eliot, "Ezra Pound," *Poetry*, Vol. LXVIII, September 1946, pp. 330−1.

12. Pound, op. cit., p. 457.

13. Ibid., p. 721.

14. Ernest Hemingway, "A Tribute to Ezra Pound," *Ezra Pound: Perspectives, essays in honor of his eightieth birthday,* ed. Noel Stock (Chicago: Henry Regnery Company, 1965), p. 151.

15. Buckminster Fuller, "How Little I Know," *And It Came to Pass − Not to Stay* (New York: Macmillan Publishing Co., 1976), pp. 1−56. First published in *Saturday Review,* vol. 49, pt. III (November 12, 1966), pp. 29−31, 67−70. See *Appendix I.*

16. Buckminster Fuller, *Nine Chains to the Moon* (New York: J. B. Lippincott, 1938).

17. Albert Einstein, "Religion and Science," *New York Times Magazine,* November 9, 1930, sec. V, p. 1.

18. J. Robert Oppenheimer's "On Albert Einstein," *Einstein: A Centenary Volume,* ed. by A. P. French (Cambridge, Massachusetts: Harvard University Press, 1979), pp. 44, 48.

19. Banesh Hoffmann, *Albert Einstein, Creator and Rebel* (New York: The Viking Press, 1972), p. 253.

20 Buckminster Fuller, "The Leonardo Type," *Earth, Inc.* (Garden City, New York: Anchor Press/Doubleday, 1973), p. 57.

21. Christopher Morley, *Chimneysmoke* (New York: George H. Doran, 1921), pp. 98–99.

22. Albert Einstein, "Autobiographical Notes," *Albert Einstein: Philosopher-Scientist,* vol. I, ed. Paul A. Schilpp (New York: Harper and Brothers, 1949), p. 5.

23. Ibid., p. 7.

24. Buckminster Fuller, *Synergetics: Explorations in the Geometry of Thinking* (New York: Macmillan Publishing Co., 1975); *Synergetics 2: Further Explorations in the Geometry of Thinking* (New York: Macmillan Publishing Co., 1979).

25. Bertrand Russel, "The Future of Mankind," *Unpopular Essays* (London: New York: Simon and Schuster, 1950), pp. 34–44; *Has Man a Future?* (New York: Simon and Schuster, 1962).

26. Buckminster Fuller, *Grunch of Giants* (New York: St. Martin's Press, 1983).

27. Albert Einstein, *Out of My Later Years* (Secaucus, New Jersey: The Citadel Press, 1956), pp. 24–30.

28. Muhammad Iqbal, *The Secrets of the Self (Asrar-i-Khudi), A Philosophical Poem,* translated from the original Persian with introduction and notes by Reynold A. Nicholson (London: Oxford University Press, 1920), p. viii. The original in Persian was first published in Lahore, 1915.

29. Ibid., p. 28.

30. Muhammad Iqbal, *The Mysteries of Selflessness (Rumuz-i-Bekhudi), A Philosophical Poem,* translated with introduction and notes by A. J. Arberry (London: John Murray, 1953), p. 62. The original in Persian was first published in Lahore, 1918.

31. Muhammad Iqbal, *Javid Nama,* translated from the Persian with introduction and notes by A. J. Arberry (London: George Allen and Unwin, 1966), p. 60. The original in Persian was first published in Lahore, 1932.

32. Muhammad Iqbal, *The Reconstruction of Religious Thought in Islam* (Lahore, 1930), pp. 8–12.

33. Pierre Teilhard de Chardin, *The Phenomenon of Man,* translated by Bernard Wall (New York: Harper and Row, 1959), pp. 264–68.

34. Martin Buber, *I and Thou,* translated by Walter Kaufmann (New York: Charles Scribner's Sons, 1970).

35. Albert Einstein, *Out of My Later Years* (Secaucus, New Jersey: The Citadel Press, 1956), pp. 24–25.

36. See Buckminster Fuller's "Mistake Mystique," *Appendix III.*

37. Iqbal, *Javid Nama,* p. 60.

38. Buckminster Fuller, *Critical Path* (New York: St. Martin's Press, 1981).

# Index

108−11; "Mistake Mystique," 215−22; *Nine Chains to the Moon*, 11, 38−43; *Operating Manual for Spaceship Earth*, 15; "Preparing For a Small One-Town World," 207−13; *Synergetics*, 12

Galbraith, John, 14
Galileo Galilei, 71
Gandhi, Indira, 15−16, 35−37
Gandhi, Mahatma, 15
Genius, 59−60, 82−84, 96
Geodesic dome, 13−14, 86−88, 112−16
God, 38, 39, 92−96, 100, 107−11, 118−28, 149, 155, 157
Goddard, Robert H., 100−101
Gravity and radiation, 100−106, 125−27
*Grunch of Giants,* 85

Hahn, Otto, 45
Hemingway, Ernest, 28
Hoffmann, Banesh, 48
Hope, 85−93, 97, 100
"How Little I Know," 29−34, 161−205
Hubble, Edwin Powell, 42
*Humans in Universe,* 17, 139−140

"Integrity," 223−28
Intellectual Development Game, 31−33
*Intuition*, 20, 25, 73, 75, 109−11
Intuition, 73−80, 146
Iqbal, Muhammad, 118−121, 137

Jeans, James Hopwood, Sir, 67

Kepler, Johannes, 39, 71, 90, 94
Khrushchev, Nikita, 13−14
Kipling, Rudyard, 157

Leonardo da Vinci, 82−83; mentioned 12, 20, 73, 76, 78, 85, 96

Leonardo Type, 16, 49
Love, 97, 100, 106−21, 124−27, 135−37
Luce, Claire Booth, 16−17

McCready's "gossamer albatross," 88
Mach, Ernst, 67−68
MacLeish, Archibald, 17
Malthus, Thomas, 86, 95
Manhattan Project, 44−48, 124−25
Medal of Freedom, 17
Meitner, Lisa, 45
Minnesota, University of, 15
"Mistake Mystique," 215−22
Montreal World Fair, 112−16. *See also* Geodesic dome
Morgan, Priscilla, 22
Morley, Christopher, 41, 50−51
Moynihan, Patrick, 14
Mrs. Murphy's Horse Power, 43

Nehru, Jawaharlal, 15
Nehru Memorial Lecture, Third, 15−16, 49, 82
Newton, Isaac, Sir, 12, 39, 40, 71, 100−101
*Nine Chains to the Moon,* 11, 38−43
Noguchi, Isamu, 21−23
Northrop, F. S. C., 74−75
Nothingness, symbol of, 68

*Operating Manual for Spaceship Earth,* 15
Oppenheimer, J. Robert, 44−45

Pantheon, 87
Paracelsus, Philippus Aureolus, 12
Pauling, Linus, 62
People's Republic of China, 14−15
Poetry, 20−21, 24−37, 50−54, 107−11
Polyhedra, 64−72
Polyvertexia, 67, 69, 70
"Post-moon-landers," 133−34

234

Pound, Ezra, 20–29, 30, 33, 49
"Preparing For a Small One-Town
    World," 207–13
Princeton University, 49

Radhakrishnan, S., 123
Radiation, *see* Gravity and radiation
Religion, 38–39, 93–96, 107–108,
    118–24
Rembrandt van Rijn, 70, 71
Rockefeller, David, 14
Roosevelt, Eleanor, 11
Roosevelt, Franklin D., 45–47
Rudge, Olga, 20–25
Russell, Bertrand, 85, 93

Saint Peter's Dome, 87
Simon, Norton, 14
Snyder, Alexandra, 53–54
Snyder, Allegra Fuller, 53–55, 112
Snyder, Jamie Lawrence, 53-54
Spaceship Earth, 13, 157–59
Spinoza, Baruch, 38, 121
Spoleto Festival, 20–21
Strassmann, Fritz, 45
Structural systems, 57, 62–63,
    64–72, 81–84, 86–90. *See also*
    Gravity and radiation; Syn-
    ergetics; Technology; Tensegrity;
    Vectors
Students, dissident, 132–33
Suzuki, D. T., 124
*Synergetics,* 12
Synergetics, 12, 84, 125–27

Tagore, Rabindranath, 51–53, 137
Taj Mahal, 122–26
Technology, 86–90, 92–93, 129,
    133, 158–59
Teilhard de Chardin, Pierre, 121,
    122–23
Tensegrity, 49, 89, 90
Tentative Cosmic Inventory, 42
Tesla, Nicola, 12
Tetrahedron, 36, 62, 67, 72, 82
Tetravertexion, 68, 69, 70, 72
Thinking process, 19–20, 60–63,
    65–66, 71–72, 73, 76–84
Thought systems, 65–66, 71–72
Triangles, 81–82

United States International Uni-
    versity, 17, 56
Universe, 30–34, 37, 49, 57, 65–68
    *passim,* 82, 87, 112, 119–21,
    127, 129–30, 149; mentioned 16,
    94, 119, 157
USSR, 13–14, 73
U Thant, 12

Van't Hoff, Jacobus Hendricus,
    62–63
Vectors, 102–106

Wells, H. G., 11
Whitman, Walt, 27
Woman, 135–37, 145
Wright, Frank Lloyd, 11